GLUTEN, SOY, AND DAIRY-FREE
COOKBOOK

Allergy-Free, Delicious, and Nutritious Recipes for a Healthy Lifestyle

Brian Wilson

CONTENT

INTRODUCTION..**1**

Gluten, Soy, and Dairy-Free food list........................**4**

Smart Shopping Tips for Gluten, Soy, and Dairy-Free Foods 9

Gluten, Soy, and Dairy-Free Breakfast Recipes...................**13**

Quinoa Breakfast Bowl 13

Sweet Potato Hash with Eggs.....................................14

Gluten-Free Banana Pancakes 15

Chia Seed Pudding 16

Avocado Toast with Tomato and Basil 16

Fruit and Nut Smoothie Bowl......................................17

Egg and Vegetable Muffins...18

Coconut and Berry Parfait 19

Pumpkin Spice Smoothie 19

Almond Butter and Banana Overnight Oats................20

Raspberry Almond Chia Pudding Parfait 21

Sunflower Seed Butter Banana Smoothie 22

Spinach and Tomato Frittata..23

Blueberry Coconut Flour Pancakes 24

Breakfast Stuffed Sweet Potatoes................................24

Pineapple and Coconut Chia Smoothie Bowl..............25

Savory Quinoa Breakfast Bowl 26

Cinnamon Raisin Overnight Oats................................27

Zucchini and Tomato Egg Muffins 27

Chocolate Banana Protein Smoothie 28

Acai Berry Bowl..29

Chickpea Flour Pancakes...30

Mango Coconut Chia Pudding Parfait 31

Breakfast Tacos with Scrambled Tofu 31

Peach and Raspberry Breakfast Smoothie 32

Sesame Ginger Tofu Scramble 33

Apple Cinnamon Quinoa Bowl 34

Cauliflower Breakfast Hash 35

Banana Almond Butter Overnight Oats 35

Strawberry Coconut Flour Muffins 36

Gluten, Soy, and Dairy-Free Lunch Recipes 38

Grilled Chicken and Quinoa Salad 38

Lentil and Vegetable Stir-Fry 39

Quinoa Stuffed Bell Peppers 40

Chickpea and Vegetable Curry 41

Turkey Lettuce Wraps 42

Salmon and Quinoa Bowl 43

Shrimp and Avocado Salad 44

Eggplant and Chickpea Buddha Bowl 45

Teriyaki Tofu Stir-Fry 45

Mediterranean Quinoa Salad 46

Asian-Inspired Quinoa Bowl 47

Zucchini Noodles with Pesto and Cherry Tomatoes 48

Quinoa and Black Bean Stuffed Peppers 49

Sweet Potato and Chickpea Buddha Bowl 50

Thai-Inspired Tofu Salad 51

Cauliflower Rice Burrito Bowl 52

Lemon Herb Grilled Shrimp Salad 53

Cilantro Lime Chicken Bowl 53

Moroccan-Inspired Chickpea Tagine 54

Spinach and Mushroom Quiche with Almond Flour Crust.........55

Gluten, Soy, and Dairy-Free Dinner Recipes 57

Grilled Lemon Herb Chicken with Quinoa 57

Lentil and Vegetable Stir-Fry.................58

Quinoa and Black Bean Stuffed Bell Peppers 59

Teriyaki Salmon with Vegetable Quinoa 60

Chickpea and Vegetable Curry.................60

Shrimp and Avocado Salad 61

Quinoa Stuffed Portobello Mushrooms.................62

Thai Basil Chicken Stir-Fry.................63

Eggplant and Chickpea Tagine.................64

Quinoa and Vegetable Paella.................65

Lemon Garlic Shrimp with Zucchini Noodles 66

Mediterranean Stuffed Peppers 67

Teriyaki Tofu Stir-Fry with Brown Rice.................68

Sweet Potato and Chickpea Curry 69

Quinoa and Roasted Vegetable Salad.................70

Cauliflower Rice Stir-Fry with Tofu 71

Quinoa and Black Bean Enchilada Casserole 72

Moroccan Spiced Chicken with Cucumber Salad.................73

Vegan Butternut Squash and Sage Risotto 74

Thai Peanut Tofu and Vegetable Skewers.................75

Lemon Herb Baked Cod with Quinoa 75

Vegan Cauliflower Alfredo with Zoodles 76

Stuffed Acorn Squash with Quinoa and Cranberries.................77

Greek-inspired Chicken Souvlaki Bowl.................78

Spaghetti Squash Primavera 79

Sesame Ginger Tofu Stir-Fry 80

Vegan Mushroom and Spinach Risotto 81

BBQ Chickpea and Sweet Potato Skewers 82

Quinoa and Broccoli Casserole 83

Thai Red Curry with Tofu and Vegetables 84

Gluten, Soy, and Dairy-Free Snack Recipes 86

Almond Butter Energy Bites 86

Roasted Chickpeas 87

Fruit and Nut Trail Mix 88

Guacamole Stuffed Cucumber Bites 88

Rice Cake with Almond Butter and Banana Slices 89

Baked Sweet Potato Chips 90

Hummus and Veggie Snack Plate 91

Quinoa and Chia Seed Pudding Cups 91

Cinnamon Roasted Almonds 92

Avocado and Salsa Rice Cakes 93

Pumpkin Spice Energy Balls 94

Dairy-Free Spinach Artichoke Dip 95

Mango Salsa with Jicama Chips 95

Cucumber Roll-Ups with Avocado and Turkey 96

Vegan Chocolate Avocado Mousse 97

Sunflower Seed and Cranberry Bars 98

Greek Salad Skewers 99

Buffalo Cauliflower Bites 100

Apple Nachos 101

Mediterranean Stuffed Mini Peppers 101

Gluten, Soy, and Dairy-Free Dessert Recipes 103

Flourless Chocolate Avocado Brownies 103

Vegan Raspberry Almond Tart 104

Coconut Mango Chia Pudding 105

No-Bake Almond Joy Energy Bites 106

Paleo Lemon Blueberry Bars..107

Chocolate Banana Ice Cream 108

Vegan Pumpkin Pie Pudding..109

Coconut Flour Chocolate Chip Cookies.................................110

Dairy-Free Matcha Chia Seed Pudding..................................111

Gluten-Free Vegan Apple Crisp...111

Quinoa Chocolate Pudding Parfait 112

Dairy-Free Chocolate Mousse...113

Gluten-Free Vegan Banana Bread..114

Raspberry Coconut Chia Seed Popsicles................................115

Chocolate Covered Strawberry Bliss Balls 116

Almond Flour Lemon Poppy Seed Cookies 117

Dairy-Free Mango Sorbet..118

Hazelnut Chocolate Banana Bites 119

Blueberry Coconut Rice Pudding...120

Vegan Chocolate Pomegranate Cups 121

Gluten, Soy, and Dairy-Free Beverage Recipes 122

Tropical Green Smoothie..122

Golden Turmeric Latte 123

Berry Beet Detox Juice..124

Iced Vanilla Almond Chai Latte...124

Cucumber Mint Cooler...125

Pineapple Ginger Elixir 126

Matcha Coconut Frappe...127

Watermelon Mint Refresher 128

Blueberry Basil Lemonade 129

Apple Cinnamon Spice Tea..129

Chilled Lavender Lemonade 130

Minty Watermelon Lime Splash 131

Raspberry Hibiscus Iced Tea..132

Energizing Green Tea Smoothie 133

Pineapple Basil Sparkler..134

Detoxifying Ginger Lemon Elixir 135

Peach Basil Iced Tea...136

Citrusy Mango Tango Smoothie 137

Blueberry Lavender Lemon Sparkle 138

Hibiscus Mint Cooler 138

Conclusion...**140**

INTRODUCTION

The significance of crafting a cookbook dedicated to gluten, soy, and dairy-free recipes transcends the boundaries of mere gastronomy. Gluten, a protein found in wheat, barley, and rye, has gained notoriety for its adverse effects on individuals with gluten sensitivities or celiac disease. Soy and dairy, omnipresent in countless recipes, can pose significant health challenges for those with allergies or intolerances to these ingredients. The journey toward a balanced and allergen-conscious lifestyle beckons for a comprehensive solution, and it is within the pages of the "Gluten, Soy, and Dairy-Free Cookbook" that this solution unfolds.

For those who navigate the intricate landscape of food allergies, understanding the potential health implications becomes paramount. Gluten, often celebrated for its elasticity in baking and revered for its role in shaping culinary delights, can be a silent adversary for a considerable segment of the population. Individuals with celiac disease, an autoimmune disorder triggered by gluten consumption, face a cascade of health issues ranging from gastrointestinal distress to malabsorption of nutrients. Gluten sensitivity, a milder form of intolerance, can manifest as a range of symptoms, including bloating, headaches, and fatigue, underscoring the importance of gluten-conscious choices in everyday meals.

Soy, another ubiquitous ingredient, is a common allergen that can elicit adverse reactions in those who are sensitive. Often used as a protein substitute in vegetarian and vegan diets, soy allergies can pose challenges for individuals seeking plant-based alternatives. The manifestation of soy allergies varies, encompassing symptoms like hives, digestive discomfort, and in severe cases, anaphylaxis.

Navigating a world filled with soy-based products demands a vigilant approach, urging individuals to scrutinize ingredient lists and seek culinary alternatives that celebrate flavor without compromising health.

Dairy, a staple in many traditional cuisines, is a source of nourishment for some but a source of distress for others. Lactose intolerance, the inability to digest lactose, the sugar found in milk, is a prevalent condition affecting a significant portion of the global population. The symptoms of lactose intolerance range from mild discomfort to severe digestive distress, emphasizing the importance of dairy-free alternatives. Additionally, some individuals may experience allergic reactions to specific proteins in dairy, such as casein and whey, further necessitating the adoption of a dairy-free lifestyle.

The "Gluten, Soy, and Dairy-Free Cookbook" emerges as a beacon of hope for those navigating the intricate web of food allergies and intolerances. Beyond being a mere compilation of recipes, this cookbook is a testament to the transformative power of culinary innovation in the face of dietary restrictions. Here, the culinary journey is not confined by limitations but is rather a celebration of diverse flavors, textures, and aromas that go beyond the traditional confines of gluten, soy, and dairy-laden recipes.

As we delve into the pages of this cookbook, we embark on a culinary odyssey that redefines what it means to create meals that are both delicious and health-conscious. Each recipe is a testament to the creative prowess that arises when one embraces the challenge of crafting dishes that cater to a spectrum of dietary needs. Whether you're a seasoned chef or a novice in the kitchen, the "Gluten, Soy, and Dairy-Free Cookbook" invites you to savor the joy of cooking without compromise, exploring a world of ingredients that not only nourish the body but also tantalize the taste buds.

In the following chapters, we will explore a diverse array of recipes that span breakfast, lunch, dinner, and delectable desserts. From hearty mains to innovative snacks, the cookbook is a treasure trove of culinary delights that invite you to savor the abundance of a gluten, soy, and dairy-free lifestyle. Each recipe is a testament to the principle that dietary restrictions need not be a hindrance but rather an opportunity for culinary exploration and innovation.

In a world where the intersection of health and taste is paramount, the "Gluten, Soy, and Dairy-Free Cookbook" stands as a guide, beckoning all those with dietary sensitivities to embrace the joy of cooking, one allergen-free recipe at a time. Let this cookbook be your trusted companion on a journey toward a healthier, more inclusive, and indulgent approach to food—an approach that proves that eliminating certain ingredients does not equate to sacrificing flavor, but rather opens the door to a world of culinary possibilities that nourish both body and soul.

CHAPTER ONE

GLUTEN, SOY, AND DAIRY-FREE FOOD LIST

Below is a diverse food list that is free from gluten, soy, and dairy. This list includes a variety of fruits, vegetables, proteins, grains, and snacks to help you create delicious and allergen-friendly meals:

Fruits:

1. Apples

2. Bananas

3. Berries (strawberries, blueberries, raspberries)

4. Oranges

5. Mangoes

6. Pineapple

7. Grapes

8. Watermelon

9. Kiwi

10. Avocado

Vegetables:

11. Broccoli

12. Carrots

13. Spinach

14. Bell peppers

15. Zucchini

16. Sweet potatoes

17. Cauliflower

18. Cucumbers

19. Tomatoes

20. Green beans

Proteins:

21. Chicken (fresh, not marinated)

22. Turkey

23. Beef

24. Pork

25. Fish (salmon, tilapia, cod)

26. Eggs

27. Tofu (ensure it's soy-free)

28. Lentils

29. Quinoa

30. Nuts (almonds, walnuts, cashews)

Grains:

31. Rice

32. Oats (certified gluten-free)

33. Millet

34. Buckwheat

35. Sorghum

36. Amaranth

37. Teff

38. Arrowroot

39. Coconut flour

40. Cassava flour

Dairy-Free Alternatives:

41. Almond milk

42. Coconut milk

43. Rice milk

44. Oat milk (ensure it's gluten-free)

45. Cashew milk

46. Dairy-free yogurt

47. Dairy-free cheese

48. Dairy-free butter

49. Coconut oil

50. Avocado oil

Snacks:

51. Popcorn

52. Rice cakes

53. Nut butter (almond, cashew)

54. Hummus

55. Guacamole

56. Veggie chips

57. Gluten-free pretzels

58. Dark chocolate (check for allergen information)

59. Rice crackers

60. Fresh fruit slices with nut butter

Condiments and Sauces:

61. Olive oil

62. Balsamic vinegar

63. Mustard (check for soy)

64. Salsa

65. Pesto (ensure it's nut-free)

66. Coconut aminos (soy sauce alternative)

67. Guacamole

68. Hot sauce (check ingredients)

69. Dairy-free mayonnaise

70. Homemade vinaigrette dressings

Beverages:

71. Herbal tea

72. Green tea

73. Black tea

74. Coffee

75. 100% fruit juices (without added sugars)

76. Coconut water

77. Sparkling water

78. Almond milk lattes

79. Smoothies (made with dairy-free alternatives)

80. Water with lemon or cucumber slices

Desserts:

81. Gluten-free and dairy-free cookies

82. Sorbet

83. Dairy-free ice cream

84. Chia seed pudding

85. Coconut milk-based desserts

86. Fruit salads

87. Gluten-free and dairy-free cakes

88. Dark chocolate (check for allergen information)

89. Energy balls (made with gluten-free oats)

90. Poached or baked fruit

This comprehensive food list provides a foundation for creating diverse and flavorful meals while adhering to a gluten, soy, and dairy-free lifestyle.

Smart Shopping Tips for Gluten, Soy, and Dairy-Free Foods

Shopping for gluten, soy, and dairy-free foods can be a rewarding and health-conscious endeavor. Here are some smart shopping tips to help you navigate the aisles and make informed choices:

1. **Read Labels Thoroughly:**

    - Scrutinize ingredient lists for gluten-containing grains (wheat, barley, rye), soy, and dairy.

    - Be cautious of hidden sources of gluten, such as modified food starch, hydrolyzed vegetable protein, and certain flavorings.

2. **Choose Certified Products:**

    - Look for certifications such as "Gluten-Free," which ensures that the product meets strict gluten-free standards.

- Check for soy-free and dairy-free labels or certifications to ensure the product aligns with your dietary needs.

3. **Explore Alternative Grains:**

   - Experiment with gluten-free grains like quinoa, rice, millet, and sorghum.

   - Try gluten-free flours such as almond flour, coconut flour, or cassava flour for baking.

4. **Opt for Fresh Produce:**

   - Emphasize fresh fruits and vegetables in your shopping cart to create vibrant, nutrient-rich meals.

   - Minimize reliance on processed foods by incorporating a variety of colorful produce into your diet.

5. **Select Lean Proteins:**

   - Choose fresh meats, poultry, and fish without added marinades or sauces containing gluten, soy, or dairy.

   - Explore plant-based protein sources like lentils, beans, and nuts.

6. **Dairy-Free Alternatives:**

   - Explore dairy-free milk alternatives like almond, coconut, or oat milk.

- Look for dairy-free yogurt, cheese, and butter made from plant-based ingredients.

7. **Beware of Soy:**

- Check labels for soy and soy derivatives, as soy can be present in various processed foods.

- Opt for soy-free alternatives, such as coconut aminos instead of soy sauce.

8. **Stock Up on Gluten-Free Snacks:**

- Keep a supply of gluten-free snacks like popcorn, rice cakes, and nut butter for quick and satisfying treats.

- Look for gluten-free and dairy-free versions of your favorite snacks.

9. **Utilize Online Resources:**

- Explore online resources and apps that provide information about gluten, soy, and dairy-free products.

- Consider using barcode scanning apps to check product details while in-store.

10. **Plan Ahead:**

- Create a weekly meal plan to streamline your shopping experience and reduce the risk of impulse purchases.

- Prepare a shopping list based on your planned meals to stay focused on your dietary goals.

11. **Ask for Assistance:**

- If unsure about a product, don't hesitate to ask store staff for assistance.

- Inquire about gluten-free, soy-free, and dairy-free options at your local grocery store.

12. Be Wary of Cross-Contamination:

- When purchasing items from the deli or bulk bins, be cautious of potential cross-contamination.

- Check if gluten-free products are stored separately to avoid the risk of contamination.

By incorporating these smart shopping tips, you can confidently select gluten, soy, and dairy-free foods that align with your dietary preferences and contribute to a healthy and enjoyable eating experience.

CHAPTER TWO

GLUTEN, SOY, AND DAIRY-FREE BREAKFAST RECIPES

When curating these breakfast recipes, meticulous attention was given to ensuring they are not only delicious but also completely free from gluten, soy, and dairy. Each recipe is crafted with thoughtfully chosen ingredients, offering a diverse range of flavors and textures to suit various tastes. Whether you're seeking a quick grab-and-go option or a leisurely weekend brunch, these recipes cater to your dietary needs without compromising on taste.

Quinoa Breakfast Bowl

Ingredients:

- 1 cup cooked quinoa
- 1/2 cup fresh berries (strawberries, blueberries)
- 1 tablespoon chopped nuts (almonds or walnuts)
- 1 tablespoon maple syrup
- 1/2 teaspoon cinnamon

Instructions:

1. In a bowl, combine cooked quinoa, fresh berries, and chopped nuts.
2. Drizzle with maple syrup and sprinkle with cinnamon.
3. Mix well and enjoy!

Preparation Time: 10 minutes

Servings: 1

Nutritional Information:

Calories: 350 | Protein: 8g | Carbohydrates: 60g | Fat: 10g | Fiber: 7g

Sweet Potato Hash with Eggs

Ingredients:

- 1 medium sweet potato, grated
- 2 eggs
- 1 tablespoon olive oil
- Salt and pepper to taste
- Fresh herbs for garnish (optional)

Instructions:

1. Heat olive oil in a skillet over medium heat.
2. Add grated sweet potato and sauté until golden brown.
3. Make two wells in the hash and crack eggs into them.
4. Cover and cook until eggs are done to your liking.
5. Season with salt and pepper, garnish with fresh herbs, and serve.

Preparation Time: 15 minutes

Servings: 2

Nutritional Information:

Calories: 280 | Protein: 10g | Carbohydrates: 25g | Fat: 15g | Fiber: 4g

Gluten-Free Banana Pancakes

Ingredients:

- 1 cup gluten-free flour

- 1 ripe banana, mashed

- 1 cup almond milk

- 1 tablespoon maple syrup

- 1 teaspoon baking powder

Instructions:

1. In a bowl, whisk together flour, mashed banana, almond milk, maple syrup, and baking powder.

2. Heat a griddle or non-stick pan over medium heat.

3. Pour 1/4 cup of batter for each pancake and cook until bubbles form, then flip.

4. Cook until golden brown and serve with your favorite toppings.

Preparation Time: 20 minutes

Servings: 2

Nutritional Information:

Calories: 220 | Protein: 4g | Carbohydrates: 40g | Fat: 5g | Fiber: 3g

Chia Seed Pudding

Ingredients:

- 2 tablespoons chia seeds
- 1/2 cup coconut milk
- 1/2 teaspoon vanilla extract
- Fresh fruit for topping

Instructions:

1. In a jar, mix chia seeds, coconut milk, and vanilla extract.
2. Stir well and refrigerate overnight or for at least 4 hours.
3. Top with fresh fruit before serving.

Preparation Time: 5 minutes (plus chilling time)

Servings: 1

Nutritional Information:

Calories: 180 | Protein: 4g | Carbohydrates: 15g | Fat: 12g | Fiber: 8g

Avocado Toast with Tomato and Basil

Ingredients:

- 1 slice gluten-free bread
- 1/2 ripe avocado, mashed
- 1 tomato, sliced
- Fresh basil leaves

- Salt and pepper to taste

Instructions:

1. Toast the gluten-free bread slice.

2. Spread mashed avocado on the toast.

3. Top with tomato slices, fresh basil, salt, and pepper.

Preparation Time: 10 minutes

Servings: 1

Nutritional Information:

Calories: 220 | Protein: 4g | Carbohydrates: 20g | Fat: 15g | Fiber: 6g

Fruit and Nut Smoothie Bowl

Ingredients:

- 1 cup mixed frozen fruits (berries, mango, pineapple)

- 1/2 banana

- 1/2 cup almond milk

- 1 tablespoon chia seeds

- Toppings: sliced almonds, shredded coconut

Instructions:

1. Blend frozen fruits, banana, and almond milk until smooth.

2. Pour into a bowl and top with chia seeds, sliced almonds, and shredded coconut.

Preparation Time: 10 minutes

Servings: 1

Nutritional Information:

Calories: 300 | Protein: 5g | Carbohydrates: 40g | Fat: 15g | Fiber: 10g

Egg and Vegetable Muffins

Ingredients:

- 4 eggs

- 1/2 cup diced bell peppers

- 1/4 cup diced onions

- Handful of spinach, chopped

- Salt and pepper to taste

Instructions:

1. Preheat the oven to 350°F (175°C).

2. In a bowl, whisk eggs and stir in diced vegetables, salt, and pepper.

3. Pour the mixture into muffin cups.

4. Bake for 15-20 minutes or until eggs are set.

Preparation Time: 25 minutes

Servings: 2

Nutritional Information:

Calories: 180 | Protein: 12g | Carbohydrates: 6g | Fat: 12g | Fiber: 2g

Coconut and Berry Parfait

Ingredients:

- 1 cup dairy-free coconut yogurt

- 1/2 cup mixed berries (strawberries, blueberries)

- 2 tablespoons gluten-free granola

- Drizzle of honey or maple syrup (optional)

Instructions:

1. In a glass, layer coconut yogurt, mixed berries, and gluten-free granola.

2. Repeat the layers.

3. Drizzle with honey or maple syrup if desired.

Preparation Time: 10 minutes

Servings: 1

Nutritional Information:

Calories: 250 | Protein: 5g | Carbohydrates: 30g | Fat: 12g | Fiber: 6g

Pumpkin Spice Smoothie

Ingredients:

- 1/2 cup canned pumpkin puree

- 1 banana

- 1/2 cup almond milk

- 1/2 teaspoon pumpkin spice

- Ice cubes

Instructions:

1. Blend pumpkin puree, banana, almond milk, pumpkin spice, and ice cubes until smooth.

2. Pour

into a glass and sprinkle a dash of additional pumpkin spice on top if desired.

Preparation Time: 5 minutes

Servings: 1

Nutritional Information:

Calories: 180 | Protein: 3g | Carbohydrates: 40g | Fat: 2g | Fiber: 8g

Almond Butter and Banana Overnight Oats

Ingredients:

- 1/2 cup gluten-free oats

- 1/2 cup almond milk

- 1 tablespoon almond butter

- 1/2 banana, sliced

- 1 teaspoon chia seeds

Instructions:

1. In a jar, combine oats, almond milk, almond butter, banana slices, and chia seeds.

2. Stir well, cover, and refrigerate overnight.

3. In the morning, give it a good stir and enjoy.

Preparation Time: 5 minutes (plus chilling time)

Servings: 1

Nutritional Information:

Calories: 350 | Protein: 10g | Carbohydrates: 45g | Fat: 15g | Fiber: 9g

Raspberry Almond Chia Pudding Parfait

Ingredients:

- 3 tablespoons chia seeds

- 1 cup almond milk

- 1/2 teaspoon almond extract

- 1/2 cup fresh raspberries

- 2 tablespoons sliced almonds

Instructions:

1. In a bowl, mix chia seeds, almond milk, and almond extract. Let it sit in the refrigerator for at least 2 hours or overnight.

2. Layer the chia pudding with fresh raspberries and sliced almonds in a glass.

3. Repeat the layers and serve chilled.

Preparation Time: 10 minutes (plus chilling time)

Servings: 1

Nutritional Information:

Calories: 280 | Protein: 8g | Carbohydrates: 30g | Fat: 15g | Fiber: 12g

Sunflower Seed Butter Banana Smoothie

Ingredients:

- 1 ripe banana
- 2 tablespoons sunflower seed butter
- 1 cup coconut milk
- Ice cubes
- Pinch of cinnamon

Instructions:

1. Blend banana, sunflower seed butter, coconut milk, and ice cubes until smooth.

2. Pour into a glass, sprinkle with a pinch of cinnamon, and enjoy.

Preparation Time: 5 minutes

Servings: 1

Nutritional Information:

Calories: 320 | Protein: 5g | Carbohydrates: 30g | Fat: 22g | Fiber: 6g

Spinach and Tomato Frittata

Ingredients:

- 4 eggs

- 1 cup fresh spinach, chopped

- 1 tomato, diced

- 1/4 cup nutritional yeast

- Salt and pepper to taste

Instructions:

1. Preheat the oven to 375°F (190°C).

2. Whisk eggs and mix in chopped spinach, diced tomato, nutritional yeast, salt, and pepper.

3. Pour the mixture into a greased baking dish and bake for 20-25 minutes or until set.

4. Slice and serve.

Preparation Time: 30 minutes

Servings: 4

Nutritional Information:

Calories: 150 | Protein: 12g | Carbohydrates: 5g | Fat: 8g | Fiber: 2g

Blueberry Coconut Flour Pancakes

Ingredients:

- 1/2 cup coconut flour

- 1/2 teaspoon baking powder

- 2 eggs

- 1/2 cup almond milk

- 1/2 cup fresh blueberries

Instructions:

1. In a bowl, mix coconut flour, baking powder, eggs, and almond milk until well combined.

2. Gently fold in fresh blueberries.

3. Cook pancakes on a griddle or non-stick pan until golden brown.

Preparation Time: 15 minutes

Servings: 2

Nutritional Information:

Calories: 220 | Protein: 10g | Carbohydrates: 20g | Fat: 10g | Fiber: 8g

Breakfast Stuffed Sweet Potatoes

Ingredients:

- 2 medium sweet potatoes, baked

- 1/2 cup cooked quinoa

- 1/4 cup black beans, rinsed and drained

- 1 avocado, sliced

- Salsa for topping

Instructions:

1. Cut baked sweet potatoes in half.

2. Fluff the insides with a fork and top with cooked quinoa, black beans, avocado slices, and salsa.

Preparation Time: 20 minutes

Servings: 2

Nutritional Information:

Calories: 300 | Protein: 8g | Carbohydrates: 40g | Fat: 15g | Fiber: 10g

Pineapple and Coconut Chia Smoothie Bowl

Ingredients:

- 1 cup frozen pineapple chunks

- 1/2 cup coconut milk

- 2 tablespoons chia seeds

- Toppings: sliced banana, shredded coconut

Instructions:

1. Blend frozen pineapple, coconut milk, and chia seeds until smooth.

2. Pour into a bowl and top with sliced banana and shredded coconut.

Preparation Time: 10 minutes

Servings: 1

Nutritional Information:

Calories: 260 | Protein: 5g | Carbohydrates: 30g | Fat: 14g | Fiber: 9g

Savory Quinoa Breakfast Bowl

Ingredients:

- 1 cup cooked quinoa
- 1/4 cup cherry tomatoes, halved
- 1/4 cup cucumber, diced
- 1/4 cup olives, sliced
- 2 tablespoons olive oil
- Salt and pepper to taste

Instructions:

1. In a bowl, combine cooked quinoa, cherry tomatoes, cucumber, olives, olive oil, salt, and pepper.

2. Mix well and serve warm.

Preparation Time: 15 minutes

Servings: 1

Nutritional Information:

Calories: 320 | Protein: 8g | Carbohydrates: 30g | Fat: 18g | Fiber: 5g

Cinnamon Raisin Overnight Oats

Ingredients:

- 1/2 cup gluten-free oats
- 1/2 cup almond milk
- 1 tablespoon raisins
- 1/2 teaspoon cinnamon
- 1 tablespoon maple syrup

Instructions:

1. In a jar, combine oats, almond milk, raisins, cinnamon, and maple syrup.

2. Stir well and refrigerate overnight.

3. In the morning, give it a good stir and enjoy.

Preparation Time: 5 minutes (plus chilling time)

Servings: 1

Nutritional Information:

Calories: 250 | Protein: 5g | Carbohydrates: 40g | Fat: 8g | Fiber: 6g

Zucchini and Tomato Egg Muffins

Ingredients:

- 4 eggs

- 1 zucchini, grated

- 1 tomato, diced

- 1/4 cup dairy-free cheese (optional)

- Salt and pepper to taste

Instructions:

1. Preheat the oven to 375°F (190°C).

2. In a bowl, whisk eggs and mix in grated zucchini, diced tomato, dairy-free cheese, salt, and pepper.

3. Pour the mixture into muffin cups.

4. Bake for 15-20 minutes or until eggs are set.

Preparation Time: 25 minutes

Servings: 2

Nutritional Information:

Calories: 180 | Protein: 12g | Carbohydrates: 5g | Fat: 12g | Fiber: 2g

Chocolate Banana Protein Smoothie
Ingredients:

- 1 banana

- 1 cup almond milk

- 1 scoop gluten-free chocolate protein powder

- 1 tablespoon almond butter

- Ice cubes

Instructions:

1. Blend banana, almond milk, chocolate protein powder, almond butter, and ice cubes until smooth.

2. Pour into a glass and enjoy the chocolaty goodness.

Preparation Time: 5 minutes

Servings: 1

Nutritional Information:

Calories: 300 | Protein: 20g | Carbohydrates: 30g | Fat: 12g | Fiber: 6g

Acai Berry Bowl

Ingredients:

- 1 pack frozen acai puree

- 1/2 banana

- 1/2 cup mixed berries (strawberries, blueberries)

- 1/4 cup gluten-free granola

- 1 tablespoon shredded coconut

Instructions:

1. Blend acai puree, banana, and mixed berries until smooth.

2. Pour into a bowl and top with gluten-free granola and shredded coconut.

Preparation Time: 10 minutes

Servings: 1

Nutritional Information:

Calories: 280 | Protein: 5g | Carbohydrates: 40g | Fat: 12g | Fiber: 8g

Chickpea Flour Pancakes

Ingredients:

- 1 cup chickpea flour

- 1/2 teaspoon baking soda

- 1/2 cup water

- 1 tablespoon olive oil

- 1/4 cup diced bell peppers

Instructions:

1. Whisk chickpea flour, baking soda, water, and olive oil until smooth.

2. Stir in diced bell peppers.

3. Cook pancakes on a griddle or non-stick pan until golden brown.

Preparation Time: 15 minutes

Servings: 2

Nutritional Information:

Calories: 220 | Protein: 10g | Carbohydrates: 25g | Fat: 10g | Fiber: 6g

Mango Coconut Chia Pudding Parfait

Ingredients:

- 3 tablespoons chia seeds

- 1 cup coconut milk

- 1/2 teaspoon vanilla extract

- 1/2 cup diced mango

- 2 tablespoons sliced almonds

Instructions:

1. Mix chia seeds, coconut milk, and vanilla extract in a bowl. Refrigerate for at least 2 hours or overnight.

2. Layer chia pudding with diced mango and sliced almonds in a glass.

3. Repeat the layers and serve chilled.

Preparation Time: 10 minutes (plus chilling time)

Servings: 1

Nutritional Information:

Calories: 300 | Protein: 7g | Carbohydrates: 30g | Fat: 18g | Fiber: 10g

Breakfast Tacos with Scrambled Tofu

Ingredients:

- 4 corn tortillas (gluten-free)

- 1/2 cup firm tofu, crumbled

- 1/4 cup diced tomatoes

- 2 tablespoons chopped cilantro

- Salsa for topping

Instructions:

1. Warm corn tortillas in a dry skillet.

2. In a separate skillet, scramble tofu until heated through.

3. Assemble tacos with scrambled tofu, diced tomatoes, cilantro, and salsa.

Preparation Time: 15 minutes

Servings: 2

Nutritional Information:

Calories: 220 | Protein: 10g | Carbohydrates: 25g | Fat: 10g | Fiber: 5g

Peach and Raspberry Breakfast Smoothie

Ingredients:

- 1 cup frozen peaches

- 1/2 cup frozen raspberries

- 1/2 cup almond milk

- 1 tablespoon hemp seeds

- 1 teaspoon honey (optional)

Instructions:

1. Blend frozen peaches, raspberries, almond milk, and hemp seeds until smooth.

2. Sweeten with honey if desired and blend again.

Preparation Time: 5 minutes

Servings: 1

Nutritional Information:

Calories: 220 | Protein: 5g | Carbohydrates: 30g | Fat: 10g | Fiber: 8g

Sesame Ginger Tofu Scramble

Ingredients:

- 1/2 cup firm tofu, crumbled
- 1 tablespoon sesame oil
- 2 tablespoons chopped green onions
- 1/4 cup diced bell peppers
- 1 teaspoon grated ginger

Instructions:

1. In a skillet, heat sesame oil over medium heat.

2. Add crumbled tofu, green onions, diced bell peppers, and grated ginger.

3. Sauté until vegetables are tender and tofu is heated through.

Preparation Time: 15 minutes

Servings: 1

Nutritional Information:

Calories: 250 | Protein: 15g | Carbohydrates: 10g | Fat: 18g | Fiber: 3g

Apple Cinnamon Quinoa Bowl

Ingredients:

- 1 cup cooked quinoa
- 1 apple, diced
- 1 tablespoon almond butter
- 1/2 teaspoon cinnamon
- 1 tablespoon chopped walnuts

Instructions:

1. In a bowl, combine cooked quinoa, diced apple, almond butter, cinnamon, and chopped walnuts.

2. Mix well and enjoy the warm, comforting flavors.

Preparation Time: 10 minutes

Servings: 1

Nutritional Information:

Calories: 320 | Protein: 7g | Carbohydrates: 45g | Fat: 12g | Fiber: 7g

Cauliflower Breakfast Hash

Ingredients:

- 2 cups cauliflower rice

- 1/4 cup diced red onion

- 1/2 cup diced bell peppers

- 1 tablespoon olive oil

- Salt and pepper to taste

Instructions:

1. In a skillet, heat olive oil over medium heat.

2. Add cauliflower rice, diced red onion, and bell peppers.

3. Sauté until cauliflower is golden brown and vegetables are tender.

Preparation Time: 15 minutes

Servings: 2

Nutritional Information:

Calories: 150 | Protein: 5g | Carbohydrates: 10g | Fat: 12g | Fiber: 4g

Banana Almond Butter Overnight Oats

Ingredients:

- 1/2 cup gluten-free oats

- 1/2 cup almond milk

- 1 tablespoon almond butter

- 1/2 banana, sliced

- 1 teaspoon chia seeds

Instructions:

1. In a jar, combine oats, almond milk, almond butter, sliced banana, and chia seeds.

2. Stir well and refrigerate overnight.

3. In the morning, give it a good stir and enjoy.

Preparation Time: 5 minutes (plus chilling time)

Servings: 1

Nutritional Information:

Calories: 280 | Protein: 7g | Carbohydrates: 40g | Fat: 12g | Fiber: 8g

Strawberry Coconut Flour Muffins

Ingredients:

- 1 cup coconut flour

- 1/2 teaspoon baking powder

- 1/2 cup coconut milk

- 1/4 cup maple syrup

- 1/2 cup diced strawberries

Instructions:

1. Preheat the oven to 350°F (175°C) and line a muffin tin with paper liners.

2. In a bowl, mix coconut flour, baking powder, coconut milk, and maple syrup until well combined.

3. Gently fold in diced strawberries.

4. Spoon the batter into muffin cups and bake for 20-25 minutes or until a toothpick comes out clean.

Preparation Time: 30 minutes

Servings: 6

Nutritional Information:

Calories: 180 | Protein: 4g | Carbohydrates: 25g | Fat: 8g | Fiber: 7g

These carefully selected gluten, soy, and dairy-free breakfast recipes not only cater to your dietary needs but also deliver a burst of flavors and nutrients. Feel free to adjust ingredients based on personal preferences and enjoy a wholesome and allergen-friendly start to your day.

CHAPTER THREE

GLUTEN, SOY, AND DAIRY-FREE LUNCH RECIPES

Each of these lunch recipes has been meticulously selected to align with a gluten, soy, and dairy-free lifestyle. Packed with wholesome ingredients and rich flavors, these meals cater to dietary needs without compromising taste. Enjoy a diverse range of dishes that make lunchtime not only delicious but also nourishing.

Grilled Chicken and Quinoa Salad

Ingredients:

- 1 cup cooked quinoa

- 6 oz grilled chicken breast, sliced

- 1 cup cherry tomatoes, halved

- 1 cucumber, diced

- 2 tablespoons olive oil

- 1 tablespoon balsamic vinegar

- Salt and pepper to taste

Instructions:

1. In a bowl, combine quinoa, grilled chicken, cherry tomatoes, and cucumber.

2. Drizzle with olive oil and balsamic vinegar.

3. Season with salt and pepper, toss gently, and serve.

Preparation Time: 20 minutes

Servings: 2

Nutritional Information:

Calories: 400 | Protein: 30g | Carbohydrates: 30g | Fat: 18g | Fiber: 5g

Lentil and Vegetable Stir-Fry

Ingredients:

- 1 cup cooked lentils

- 1 cup broccoli florets

- 1 bell pepper, sliced

- 1 carrot, julienned

- 2 tablespoons coconut aminos

- 1 tablespoon sesame oil

- 1 teaspoon minced ginger

Instructions:

1. In a wok, heat sesame oil and sauté ginger.

2. Add broccoli, bell pepper, and carrot. Stir-fry until vegetables are tender.

3. Add cooked lentils and coconut aminos. Stir until well combined.

Preparation Time: 25 minutes

Servings: 2

Nutritional Information:

Calories: 350 | Protein: 18g | Carbohydrates: 45g | Fat: 10g | Fiber: 15g

Quinoa Stuffed Bell Peppers

Ingredients:

- 2 bell peppers, halved and seeds removed
- 1 cup cooked quinoa
- 1/2 cup black beans, rinsed and drained
- 1/2 cup corn kernels
- 1/2 cup diced tomatoes
- 1 teaspoon taco seasoning
- Guacamole for topping

Instructions:

1. Preheat the oven to 375°F (190°C).
2. In a bowl, mix quinoa, black beans, corn, diced tomatoes, and taco seasoning.
3. Stuff bell peppers with the quinoa mixture and bake for 20-25 minutes.
4. Top with guacamole before serving.

Preparation Time: 30 minutes

Servings: 2

Nutritional Information:

Calories: 320 | Protein: 12g | Carbohydrates: 50g | Fat: 8g | Fiber: 10g

Chickpea and Vegetable Curry

Ingredients:

- 1 can (15 oz) chickpeas, drained and rinsed

- 1 cup cauliflower florets

- 1 cup green beans, chopped

- 1 onion, finely chopped

- 2 tablespoons curry powder

- 1 can (14 oz) coconut milk

- Salt and pepper to taste

Instructions:

1. In a pot, sauté chopped onion until translucent.

2. Add curry powder and stir. Add chickpeas, cauliflower, and green beans.

3. Pour in coconut milk, season with salt and pepper, and simmer until vegetables are tender.

Preparation Time: 35 minutes

Servings: 4

Nutritional Information:

Calories: 380 | Protein: 15g | Carbohydrates: 40g | Fat: 20g | Fiber: 10g

Turkey Lettuce Wraps

Ingredients:

- 1 lb ground turkey
- 1 tablespoon olive oil
- 1 bell pepper, diced
- 1 zucchini, diced
- 1/2 cup water chestnuts, chopped
- 2 tablespoons gluten-free soy sauce
- Iceberg lettuce leaves for wrapping

Instructions:

1. In a skillet, heat olive oil and cook ground turkey until browned.

2. Add diced bell pepper, zucchini, and water chestnuts. Sauté until vegetables are tender.

3. Stir in gluten-free soy sauce and cook for an additional 2 minutes.

4. Serve the turkey mixture in iceberg lettuce leaves.

Preparation Time: 25 minutes

Servings: 4

Nutritional Information:

Calories: 280 | Protein: 20g | Carbohydrates: 15g | Fat: 15g | Fiber: 5g

Salmon and Quinoa Bowl

Ingredients:

- 8 oz salmon fillet
- 1 cup cooked quinoa
- 1 cup steamed broccoli
- 1/4 cup sliced almonds
- 1 tablespoon lemon juice
- Salt and pepper to taste

Instructions:

1. Season the salmon fillet with salt, pepper, and lemon juice. Bake until cooked through.
2. In a bowl, combine cooked quinoa, steamed broccoli, and sliced almonds.
3. Top with the baked salmon.

Preparation Time: 30 minutes

Servings: 2

Nutritional Information:

Calories: 450 | Protein: 30g | Carbohydrates: 35g | Fat: 20g | Fiber: 8g

Shrimp and Avocado Salad

Ingredients:

- 1/2 lb shrimp, peeled and deveined

- 2 cups mixed greens

- 1 avocado, sliced

- 1 cup cherry tomatoes, halved

- 2 tablespoons balsamic vinaigrette

- Fresh cilantro for garnish

Instructions:

1. Cook shrimp in a skillet until pink and opaque.

2. In a bowl, toss mixed greens, avocado slices, and cherry tomatoes.

3. Top with cooked shrimp, drizzle with balsamic vinaigrette, and garnish with fresh cilantro.

Preparation Time: 15 minutes

Servings: 2

Nutritional Information:

Calories: 320 | Protein: 25g | Carbohydrates: 20g | Fat: 18g | Fiber: 8g

Eggplant and Chickpea Buddha Bowl

Ingredients:

- 1 small eggplant, sliced
- 1 can (15 oz) chickpeas, drained and rinsed
- 1 cup quinoa, cooked
- 1 cup kale, chopped
- 2 tablespoons tahini
- 1 tablespoon lemon juice

Instructions:

1. Roast eggplant slices in the oven until golden brown.
2. In a bowl, assemble quinoa, chickpeas, roasted eggplant, and chopped kale.
3. Drizzle with tahini and lemon juice.

Preparation Time: 30 minutes

Servings: 2

Nutritional Information:

Calories: 380 | Protein: 15g | Carbohydrates: 55g | Fat: 15g | Fiber: 12g

Teriyaki Tofu Stir-Fry

Ingredients:

- 1 block firm tofu, cubed

- 1 cup broccoli florets

- 1 bell pepper, sliced

- 1 cup snap peas

- 2 tablespoons gluten-free teriyaki sauce

- 1 tablespoon sesame oil

Instructions:

1. In a wok, heat sesame oil and stir-fry tofu until golden.

2. Add broccoli, bell pepper, and snap peas. Cook until vegetables are tender.

3. Pour gluten-free teriyaki sauce over the stir-fry and toss until well coated.

Preparation Time: 25 minutes

Servings: 2

Nutritional Information:

Calories: 320 | Protein: 20g | Carbohydrates: 30g | Fat: 15g | Fiber: 8g

Mediterranean Quinoa Salad

Ingredients:

- 1 cup cooked quinoa

- 1/2 cup cucumber, diced

- 1/2 cup cherry tomatoes, halved

- 1/4 cup Kalamata olives, sliced

- 1/4 cup red onion, finely chopped

- 2 tablespoons olive oil

- 1 tablespoon red wine vinegar

- Fresh parsley for garnish

Instructions:

1. In a bowl, combine quinoa, cucumber, cherry tomatoes, olives, and red onion.

2. Drizzle with olive oil and red wine vinegar.

3. Toss the salad and garnish with fresh parsley.

Preparation Time: 20 minutes

Servings: 2

Nutritional Information:

Calories: 350 | Protein: 10g | Carbohydrates: 40g | Fat: 18g | Fiber: 7g

Asian-Inspired Quinoa Bowl

Ingredients:

- 1 cup cooked quinoa

- 1 cup shredded cabbage

- 1 carrot, julienned

- 1/2 cup edamame, shelled

- 2 tablespoons gluten-free soy sauce

- 1 tablespoon rice vinegar

- Sesame seeds for garnish

Instructions:

1. In a bowl, combine quinoa, shredded cabbage, julienned carrot, and edamame.

2. Drizzle with gluten-free soy sauce and rice vinegar.

3. Toss the ingredients well and sprinkle sesame seeds before serving.

Preparation Time: 15 minutes

Servings: 2

Nutritional Information:

Calories: 300 | Protein: 12g | Carbohydrates: 45g | Fat: 8g | Fiber: 10g

Zucchini Noodles with Pesto and Cherry Tomatoes

Ingredients:

- 2 large zucchinis, spiralized

- 1 cup cherry tomatoes, halved

- 1/4 cup pine nuts

- 1/2 cup fresh basil leaves

- 2 tablespoons nutritional yeast

- 3 tablespoons olive oil

Instructions:

1. In a blender, combine basil, pine nuts, nutritional yeast, and olive oil. Blend into a pesto.

2. Toss zucchini noodles with pesto and cherry tomatoes.

3. Serve chilled or at room temperature.

Preparation Time: 20 minutes

Servings: 2

Nutritional Information:

Calories: 280 | Protein: 8g | Carbohydrates: 20g | Fat: 22g | Fiber: 6g

Quinoa and Black Bean Stuffed Peppers

Ingredients:

- 2 bell peppers, halved and seeds removed

- 1 cup cooked quinoa

- 1/2 cup black beans, rinsed and drained

- 1/2 cup corn kernels

- 1/4 cup diced red onion

- 1 teaspoon cumin

- Salsa for topping

Instructions:

1. Preheat the oven to 375°F (190°C).

2. In a bowl, mix quinoa, black beans, corn, diced red onion, and cumin.

3. Stuff bell peppers with the quinoa mixture and bake for 20-25 minutes.

4. Top with salsa before serving.

Preparation Time: 30 minutes

Servings: 2

Nutritional Information:

Calories: 320 | Protein: 15g | Carbohydrates: 50g | Fat: 8g | Fiber: 10g

Sweet Potato and Chickpea Buddha Bowl

Ingredients:

- 1 large sweet potato, cubed
- 1 can (15 oz) chickpeas, drained and rinsed
- 1 cup kale, chopped
- 2 tablespoons tahini
- 1 tablespoon lemon juice
- Smoked paprika for seasoning

Instructions:

1. Roast sweet potato cubes and chickpeas in the oven until golden.

2. In a bowl, assemble quinoa, roasted sweet potatoes, chickpeas, and chopped kale.

3. Drizzle with tahini, lemon juice, and sprinkle with smoked paprika.

Preparation Time: 35 minutes

Servings: 2

Nutritional Information:

Calories: 380 | Protein: 15g | Carbohydrates: 55g | Fat: 15g | Fiber: 12g

Thai-Inspired Tofu Salad

Ingredients:

- 1 block firm tofu, cubed

- 2 cups mixed greens

- 1 mango, sliced

- 1/4 cup peanuts, chopped

- 2 tablespoons gluten-free soy sauce

- 1 tablespoon lime juice

Instructions:

1. Sauté cubed tofu until golden.

2. In a bowl, combine mixed greens, sliced mango, and chopped peanuts.

3. Top with sautéed tofu and drizzle with gluten-free soy sauce and lime juice.

Preparation Time: 20 minutes

Servings: 2

Nutritional Information:

Calories: 340 | Protein: 18g | Carbohydrates: 35g | Fat: 18g | Fiber: 8g

Cauliflower Rice Burrito Bowl

Ingredients:

- 2 cups cauliflower rice

- 1 cup black beans, rinsed and drained

- 1 cup corn kernels

- 1/2 cup diced tomatoes

- 1/4 cup chopped cilantro

- Avocado slices for topping

Instructions:

1. Sauté cauliflower rice until tender.

2. In a bowl, assemble cauliflower rice, black beans, corn, diced tomatoes, and chopped cilantro.

3. Top with avocado slices before serving.

Preparation Time: 25 minutes

Servings: 2

Nutritional Information:

Calories: 290 | Protein: 12g | Carbohydrates: 40g | Fat: 10g | Fiber: 12g

Lemon Herb Grilled Shrimp Salad

Ingredients:

- 1/2 lb shrimp, peeled and deveined
- 4 cups mixed salad greens
- 1 cucumber, sliced
- 1/2 cup cherry tomatoes, halved
- 2 tablespoons olive oil
- 1 tablespoon chopped fresh herbs (such as parsley and dill)

Instructions:

1. Grill shrimp until pink and opaque.
2. In a large bowl, toss mixed salad greens, sliced cucumber, and cherry tomatoes.
3. Top with grilled shrimp, drizzle with olive oil, and sprinkle with chopped herbs.

Preparation Time: 15 minutes

Servings: 2

Nutritional Information:

Calories: 280 | Protein: 20g | Carbohydrates: 15g | Fat: 15g | Fiber: 6g

Cilantro Lime Chicken Bowl

Ingredients:

- 1 lb chicken breast, grilled and sliced

- 1 cup quinoa, cooked

- 1/2 cup black beans, rinsed and drained

- 1/2 cup corn kernels

- 1/4 cup diced red onion

- Fresh cilantro for garnish

- Lime wedges for serving

Instructions:

1. Assemble bowls with quinoa, grilled chicken, black beans, corn, and diced red onion.

2. Garnish with fresh cilantro and serve with lime wedges.

Preparation Time: 30 minutes

Servings: 2

Nutritional Information:

Calories: 380 | Protein: 30g | Carbohydrates: 40g | Fat: 12g | Fiber: 8g

Moroccan-Inspired Chickpea Tagine

Ingredients:

- 1 can (15 oz) chickpeas, drained and rinsed

- 1 cup diced butternut squash

- 1 cup diced eggplant

- 1/2 cup diced tomatoes

- 2 tablespoons olive oil

- 1 teaspoon ground cumin

- 1/2 teaspoon ground cinnamon

Instructions:

1. In a pot, sauté chickpeas, butternut squash, eggplant, and diced tomatoes in olive oil.

2. Season with ground cumin and cinnamon. Simmer until vegetables are tender.

Preparation Time: 40 minutes

Servings: 4

Nutritional Information:

Calories: 320 | Protein: 12g | Carbohydrates: 45g | Fat: 12g | Fiber: 12g

Spinach and Mushroom Quiche with Almond Flour Crust

Ingredients:

- 2 cups almond flour

- 1/4 cup coconut oil, melted

- 1/2 teaspoon salt

- 2 cups fresh spinach, chopped

- 1 cup mushrooms, sliced

- 6 large eggs

- 1 cup almond milk

- Salt and pepper to taste

Instructions:

1. Preheat the oven to 350°F (175°C).

2. Mix almond flour, melted coconut oil, and salt. Press into a pie dish for the crust.

3. Sauté spinach and mushrooms until wilted.

4. In a bowl, whisk eggs and almond milk. Season with salt and pepper.

5. Pour egg mixture over sautéed vegetables in the pie dish.

6. Bake for 30-35 minutes or until the center is set.

Preparation Time: 45 minutes

Servings: 6

Nutritional Information:

Calories: 320 | Protein: 15g | Carbohydrates: 15g | Fat: 25g | Fiber: 6g

These Lunch recipes are thoughtfully crafted to meet your gluten, soy, and dairy-free dietary preferences. Enjoy the delicious flavors and nourishing ingredients in each wholesome meal.

CHAPTER FOUR
GLUTEN, SOY, AND DAIRY-FREE DINNER RECIPES

These dinner recipes have been meticulously chosen to align with a gluten, soy, and dairy-free lifestyle. Packed with wholesome ingredients and bursting with flavor, these meals cater to dietary needs without compromising on taste. Enjoy a variety of dishes that make dinnertime not only satisfying but also nutritionally balanced.

Grilled Lemon Herb Chicken with Quinoa
Ingredients:

- 2 boneless, skinless chicken breasts

- 1 cup quinoa, uncooked

- 1 lemon (juiced)

- 2 tablespoons olive oil

- 1 teaspoon dried oregano

- 1 teaspoon dried thyme

- Salt and pepper to taste

Instructions:

1. Marinate chicken in lemon juice, olive oil, oregano, thyme, salt, and pepper.

2. Grill until chicken is cooked through.

3. Serve over a bed of cooked quinoa.

Preparation Time: 30 minutes

Servings: 2

Nutritional Information:

Calories: 400 | Protein: 30g | Carbohydrates: 30g | Fat: 18g | Fiber: 4g

Lentil and Vegetable Stir-Fry

Ingredients:

- 1 cup cooked lentils

- 1 cup broccoli florets

- 1 bell pepper, sliced

- 1 carrot, julienned

- 2 tablespoons coconut aminos

- 1 tablespoon sesame oil

- 1 teaspoon minced ginger

Instructions:

1. In a wok, heat sesame oil and sauté ginger.

2. Add broccoli, bell pepper, and carrot. Stir-fry until vegetables are tender.

3. Add cooked lentils and coconut aminos. Stir until well combined.

Preparation Time: 25 minutes

Servings: 2

Nutritional Information:

Calories: 350 | Protein: 18g | Carbohydrates: 45g | Fat: 10g | Fiber: 15g

Quinoa and Black Bean Stuffed Bell Peppers
Ingredients:

- 2 bell peppers, halved and seeds removed

- 1 cup cooked quinoa

- 1/2 cup black beans, rinsed and drained

- 1/2 cup corn kernels

- 1/2 cup diced tomatoes

- 1 teaspoon taco seasoning

- Guacamole for topping

Instructions:

1. Preheat the oven to 375°F (190°C).

2. Mix quinoa, black beans, corn, diced tomatoes, and taco seasoning.

3. Stuff bell peppers with the quinoa mixture and bake for 20-25 minutes.

4. Top with guacamole before serving.

Preparation Time: 30 minutes

Servings: 2

Nutritional Information:

Calories: 320 | Protein: 15g | Carbohydrates: 50g | Fat: 8g | Fiber: 10g

Teriyaki Salmon with Vegetable Quinoa

Ingredients:

- 2 salmon fillets
- 1 cup mixed vegetables (broccoli, snap peas, carrots)
- 1 cup quinoa, cooked
- 2 tablespoons gluten-free teriyaki sauce
- 1 tablespoon olive oil

Instructions:

1. Marinate salmon in gluten-free teriyaki sauce.
2. In a pan, sauté mixed vegetables in olive oil until crisp-tender.
3. Grill or pan-sear salmon and serve over vegetable quinoa.

Preparation Time: 30 minutes

Servings: 2

Nutritional Information:

Calories: 420 | Protein: 30g | Carbohydrates: 30g | Fat: 20g | Fiber: 8g

Chickpea and Vegetable Curry

Ingredients:

- 1 can (15 oz) chickpeas, drained and rinsed

- 1 cup cauliflower florets

- 1 cup green beans, chopped

- 1 onion, finely chopped

- 2 tablespoons curry powder

- 1 can (14 oz) coconut milk

- Salt and pepper to taste

Instructions:

1. Sauté chopped onion until translucent.

2. Add curry powder and stir. Add chickpeas, cauliflower, and green beans.

3. Pour in coconut milk, season with salt and pepper, and simmer until vegetables are tender.

Preparation Time: 35 minutes

Servings: 4

Nutritional Information:

Calories: 380 | Protein: 15g | Carbohydrates: 40g | Fat: 20g | Fiber: 10g

Shrimp and Avocado Salad

Ingredients:

- 1/2 lb shrimp, peeled and deveined

- 2 cups mixed greens

- 1 avocado, sliced

- 1 cup cherry tomatoes, halved

- 2 tablespoons balsamic vinaigrette

- Fresh cilantro for garnish

Instructions:

1. Cook shrimp until pink and opaque.

2. Toss mixed greens, avocado slices, and cherry tomatoes in a bowl.

3. Top with cooked shrimp, drizzle with balsamic vinaigrette, and garnish with cilantro.

Preparation Time: 15 minutes

Servings: 2

Nutritional Information:

Calories: 320 | Protein: 25g | Carbohydrates: 20g | Fat: 18g | Fiber: 8g

Quinoa Stuffed Portobello Mushrooms

Ingredients:

- 4 large portobello mushrooms, stems removed

- 1 cup cooked quinoa

- 1/2 cup cherry tomatoes, diced

- 1/4 cup red onion, finely chopped

- 1/4 cup fresh parsley, chopped

- 2 tablespoons balsamic glaze

Instructions:

1. Preheat the oven to 375°F (190°C).

2. Mix cooked quinoa, cherry tomatoes, red onion, and parsley in a bowl.

3. Stuff portobello mushrooms with the quinoa mixture and bake for 20-25 minutes.

4. Drizzle with balsamic glaze before serving.

Preparation Time: 30 minutes

Servings: 2

Nutritional Information:

Calories: 280 | Protein: 12g | Carbohydrates: 45g | Fat: 8g | Fiber: 8g

Thai Basil Chicken Stir-Fry

Ingredients:

- 1 lb boneless, skinless chicken thighs, sliced

- 2 cups broccoli florets

- 1 bell pepper, sliced

- 1 cup snap peas

- 2 tablespoons gluten-free soy sauce

- 1 tablespoon fish sauce

- 1 tablespoon sesame oil

- Fresh basil leaves for garnish

Instructions:

1. In a wok, stir-fry chicken until browned.

2. Add broccoli, bell pepper, and snap peas. Cook until vegetables are tender.

3. Mix in gluten-free soy sauce, fish sauce, and sesame oil.

4. Garnish with fresh basil leaves before serving.

Preparation Time: 25 minutes

Servings: 4

Nutritional Information:

Calories: 380 | Protein: 28g | Carbohydrates: 20g | Fat: 18g | Fiber: 6g

Eggplant and Chickpea Tagine

Ingredients:

- 1 small eggplant, diced

- 1 can (15 oz) chickpeas, drained and rinsed

- 1 cup diced tomatoes

- 1 onion, finely chopped

- 2 tablespoons olive oil

- 1 teaspoon ground cumin

- 1/2 teaspoon ground cinnamon

Instructions:

1. Sauté chopped onion in olive oil until translucent.

2. Add diced eggplant, chickpeas, and tomatoes. Cook until eggplant is tender.

3. Season with ground cumin and cinnamon. Simmer until flavors meld.

Preparation Time: 40 minutes

Servings: 4

Nutritional Information:

Calories: 320 | Protein: 12g | Carbohydrates: 45g | Fat: 12g | Fiber: 12g

Quinoa and Vegetable Paella

Ingredients:

- 1 cup quinoa, uncooked
- 1 onion, diced
- 1 bell pepper, diced
- 1 cup cherry tomatoes, halved
- 1 cup artichoke hearts, quartered
- 2 cloves garlic, minced
- 1 teaspoon smoked paprika
- 2 cups vegetable broth

Instructions:

1. Sauté diced onion and garlic until softened.

2. Add quinoa, bell pepper, cherry tomatoes, artichoke hearts, and smoked paprika.

3. Pour in vegetable broth and simmer until quinoa is cooked.

Preparation Time: 30 minutes

Servings: 4

Nutritional Information:

Calories: 340 | Protein: 12g | Carbohydrates: 60g | Fat: 6g | Fiber: 10g

Lemon Garlic Shrimp with Zucchini Noodles

Ingredients:

- 1/2 lb shrimp, peeled and deveined

- 4 medium zucchinis, spiralized

- 3 cloves garlic, minced

- 1 lemon (zested and juiced)

- 2 tablespoons olive oil

- Fresh parsley for garnish

Instructions:

1. Sauté shrimp in olive oil until pink and opaque.

2. Add minced garlic, lemon zest, and lemon juice. Cook for an additional minute.

3. Toss in spiralized zucchini noodles until just tender.

4. Garnish with fresh parsley before serving.

Preparation Time: 20 minutes

Servings: 2

Nutritional Information:

Calories: 280 | Protein: 20g | Carbohydrates: 15g | Fat: 15g | Fiber: 5g

Mediterranean Stuffed Peppers

Ingredients:

- 2 bell peppers, halved and seeds removed
- 1 cup cooked quinoa
- 1/2 cup chickpeas, rinsed and drained
- 1/4 cup Kalamata olives, sliced
- 1/4 cup sun-dried tomatoes, chopped
- 2 tablespoons olive oil
- Fresh basil for garnish

Instructions:

1. Preheat the oven to 375°F (190°C).
2. Mix quinoa, chickpeas, Kalamata olives, and sun-dried tomatoes.
3. Stuff bell peppers with the quinoa mixture and bake for 20-25 minutes.
4. Drizzle with olive oil and garnish with fresh basil.

Preparation Time: 30 minutes

Servings: 2

Nutritional Information:

Calories: 320 | Protein: 12g | Carbohydrates: 45g | Fat: 15g | Fiber: 8g

Teriyaki Tofu Stir-Fry with Brown Rice

Ingredients:

- 1 block firm tofu, cubed
- 1 cup broccoli florets
- 1 bell pepper, sliced
- 1 cup snap peas
- 2 tablespoons gluten-free teriyaki sauce
- 1 tablespoon sesame oil
- 1 cup brown rice, cooked

Instructions:

1. In a wok, heat sesame oil and stir-fry tofu until golden.
2. Add broccoli, bell pepper, and snap peas. Cook until vegetables are tender.
3. Pour gluten-free teriyaki sauce over the stir-fry and toss until well coated.
4. Serve over a bed of cooked brown rice.

Preparation Time: 25 minutes

Servings: 2

Nutritional Information:

Calories: 380 | Protein: 20g | Carbohydrates: 50g | Fat: 15g | Fiber: 10g

Sweet Potato and Chickpea Curry

Ingredients:

- 1 large sweet potato, diced

- 1 can (15 oz) chickpeas, drained and rinsed

- 1 onion, finely chopped

- 2 cloves garlic, minced

- 1 can (14 oz) coconut milk

- 2 tablespoons red curry paste

- Fresh cilantro for garnish

Instructions:

1. Sauté chopped onion and garlic until softened.

2. Add diced sweet potato and chickpeas. Cook until sweet potato is tender.

3. Stir in red curry paste and pour in coconut milk. Simmer until flavors meld.

4. Garnish with fresh cilantro before serving.

Preparation Time: 35 minutes

Servings: 4

Nutritional Information:

Calories: 320 | Protein: 12g | Carbohydrates: 45g | Fat: 15g | Fiber: 12g

Quinoa and Roasted Vegetable Salad

Ingredients:

- 1 cup cooked quinoa
- 1 cup cherry tomatoes, roasted
- 1 cup zucchini, diced and roasted
- 1/2 cup red bell pepper, diced
- 2 tablespoons balsamic vinaigrette
- Fresh basil for garnish

Instructions:

1. Roast cherry tomatoes and diced zucchini until caramelized.

2. In a bowl, combine quinoa, roasted vegetables, and diced red bell pepper.

3. Drizzle with balsamic vinaigrette and garnish with fresh basil.

Preparation Time: 30 minutes

Servings: 2

Nutritional Information:

Calories: 340 | Protein: 10g | Carbohydrates: 50g | Fat: 12g | Fiber: 8g

Cauliflower Rice Stir-Fry with Tofu

Ingredients:

- 1 block firm tofu, cubed

- 2 cups cauliflower rice

- 1 cup broccoli florets

- 1 carrot, julienned

- 2 tablespoons gluten-free soy sauce

- 1 tablespoon sesame oil

- Green onions for garnish

Instructions:

1. Sauté tofu in sesame oil until golden.

2. Add cauliflower rice, broccoli, and julienned carrot. Stir-fry until vegetables are tender.

3. Pour gluten-free soy sauce over the stir-fry and toss until well coated.

4. Garnish with chopped green onions before serving.

Preparation Time: 25 minutes

Servings: 2

Nutritional Information:

Calories: 320 | Protein: 18g | Carbohydrates: 25g | Fat: 15g | Fiber: 8g

Quinoa and Black Bean Enchilada Casserole

Ingredients:

- 1 cup cooked quinoa

- 1 can (15 oz) black beans, rinsed and drained

- 1 cup corn kernels

- 1 cup enchilada sauce (gluten-free)

- 1/2 cup diced green chilies

- 1 cup dairy-free shredded cheese

- Fresh cilantro for garnish

Instructions:

1. Preheat the oven to 375°F (190°C).

2. In a casserole dish, layer quinoa, black beans, corn, and green chilies.

3. Pour enchilada sauce over the layers and top with dairy-free shredded cheese.

4. Bake for 20-25 minutes until bubbly. Garnish with fresh cilantro before serving.

Preparation Time: 35 minutes

Servings: 4

Nutritional Information:

Calories: 380 | Protein: 15g | Carbohydrates: 50g | Fat: 12g | Fiber: 10g

Moroccan Spiced Chicken with Cucumber Salad

Ingredients:

- 2 chicken breasts
- 1 teaspoon ground cumin
- 1 teaspoon ground coriander
- 1/2 teaspoon ground cinnamon
- 1 cucumber, diced
- 1/4 cup red onion, finely chopped
- 2 tablespoons fresh mint, chopped
- 2 tablespoons olive oil

Instructions:

1. Rub chicken breasts with cumin, coriander, and cinnamon. Grill until cooked through.

2. In a bowl, combine diced cucumber, chopped red onion, fresh mint, and olive oil.

3. Serve grilled chicken over the cucumber salad.

Preparation Time: 30 minutes

Servings: 2

Nutritional Information:

Calories: 320 | Protein: 30g | Carbohydrates: 15g | Fat: 18g | Fiber: 5g

Vegan Butternut Squash and Sage Risotto

Ingredients:

- 1 cup Arborio rice
- 1/2 butternut squash, diced
- 1 onion, finely chopped
- 2 cloves garlic, minced
- 1/4 cup nutritional yeast
- 1/4 cup fresh sage, chopped
- 4 cups vegetable broth

Instructions:

1. Sauté chopped onion and garlic until translucent.
2. Add Arborio rice and diced butternut squash. Stir to coat in the oil.
3. Pour in vegetable broth gradually, stirring until absorbed.
4. Stir in nutritional yeast and fresh sage. Continue cooking until rice is creamy.

Preparation Time: 40 minutes

Servings: 4

Nutritional Information:

Calories: 350 | Protein: 8g | Carbohydrates: 70g | Fat: 4g | Fiber: 6g

Thai Peanut Tofu and Vegetable Skewers

Ingredients:

- 1 block firm tofu, cubed
- 1 cup broccoli florets
- 1 bell pepper, diced
- 1 zucchini, sliced
- 1/4 cup peanut sauce (gluten-free)
- Wooden skewers, soaked in water

Instructions:

1. Thread tofu, broccoli, bell pepper, and zucchini onto skewers.
2. Grill skewers until vegetables are tender and tofu is golden.
3. Brush with gluten-free peanut sauce before serving.

Preparation Time: 30 minutes
Servings: 2
Nutritional Information:
Calories: 320 | Protein: 15g | Carbohydrates: 25g | Fat: 18g | Fiber: 8g

Lemon Herb Baked Cod with Quinoa

Ingredients:

- 2 cod fillets
- 1 lemon (zested and juiced)

- 2 tablespoons olive oil

- 1 teaspoon dried thyme

- 1 teaspoon dried rosemary

- 1 cup quinoa, cooked

- Fresh parsley for garnish

Instructions:

1. Preheat the oven to 400°F (200°C).

2. Mix lemon zest, lemon juice, olive oil, thyme, and rosemary.

3. Place cod fillets on a baking sheet, drizzle with the lemon herb mixture, and bake until fish flakes easily.

4. Serve over a bed of cooked quinoa and garnish with fresh parsley.

Preparation Time: 25 minutes

Servings: 2

Nutritional Information:

Calories: 320 | Protein: 30g | Carbohydrates: 30g | Fat: 10g | Fiber: 4g

Vegan Cauliflower Alfredo with Zoodles

Ingredients:

- 1 medium cauliflower, cut into florets

- 2 cloves garlic, minced

- 1 cup unsweetened almond milk

- 1/4 cup nutritional yeast

- 2 tablespoons olive oil

- Salt and pepper to taste

- Zucchini noodles (zoodles)

Instructions:

1. Steam cauliflower until tender.

2. In a blender, combine cauliflower, minced garlic, almond milk, nutritional yeast, olive oil, salt, and pepper. Blend until smooth.

3. Toss the cauliflower Alfredo sauce with zoodles and heat until warm.

Preparation Time: 30 minutes

Servings: 2

Nutritional Information:

Calories: 250 | Protein: 8g | Carbohydrates: 20g | Fat: 15g | Fiber: 6g

Stuffed Acorn Squash with Quinoa and Cranberries

Ingredients:

- 2 acorn squashes, halved and seeds removed

- 1 cup cooked quinoa

- 1/2 cup dried cranberries

- 1/4 cup chopped pecans

- 1 tablespoon maple syrup

- Cinnamon for sprinkling

Instructions:

1. Preheat the oven to 375°F (190°C).

2. Roast acorn squashes in the oven until tender.

3. In a bowl, mix cooked quinoa, dried cranberries, chopped pecans, and maple syrup.

4. Stuff each acorn squash half with the quinoa mixture, sprinkle with cinnamon, and bake for an additional 15 minutes.

Preparation Time: 40 minutes

Servings: 4

Nutritional Information:

Calories: 280 | Protein: 6g | Carbohydrates: 50g | Fat: 8g | Fiber: 8g

Greek-inspired Chicken Souvlaki Bowl

Ingredients:

- 2 chicken breasts, grilled and sliced

- 1 cup cooked quinoa

- 1 cup cucumber, diced

- 1/2 cup cherry tomatoes, halved

- 1/4 cup red onion, thinly sliced

- 2 tablespoons Kalamata olives, sliced

- Tzatziki sauce (dairy-free)

Instructions:

1. Grill chicken breasts until cooked through and slice.

2. In a bowl, layer cooked quinoa, diced cucumber, cherry tomatoes, sliced red onion, and Kalamata olives.

3. Top with sliced chicken and drizzle with dairy-free tzatziki sauce.

Preparation Time: 30 minutes

Servings: 2

Nutritional Information:

Calories: 340 | Protein: 30g | Carbohydrates: 30g | Fat: 12g | Fiber: 6g

Spaghetti Squash Primavera

Ingredients:

- 1 spaghetti squash, halved and seeds removed

- 1 cup cherry tomatoes, halved

- 1 cup broccoli florets

- 1/2 cup bell peppers, sliced

- 2 cloves garlic, minced

- 2 tablespoons olive oil

- Fresh basil for garnish

Instructions:

1. Roast spaghetti squash in the oven until strands can be easily pulled with a fork.

2. In a pan, sauté cherry tomatoes, broccoli, bell peppers, and minced garlic in olive oil.

3. Toss spaghetti squash strands with the vegetable mixture.

4. Garnish with fresh basil before serving.

Preparation Time: 40 minutes

Servings: 2

Nutritional Information:

Calories: 280 | Protein: 6g | Carbohydrates: 35g | Fat: 15g | Fiber: 8g

Sesame Ginger Tofu Stir-Fry

Ingredients:

- 1 block firm tofu, cubed

- 2 cups snow peas

- 1 carrot, julienned

- 1 cup broccoli florets

- 2 tablespoons gluten-free soy sauce

- 1 tablespoon sesame oil

- 1 tablespoon rice vinegar

- Sesame seeds for garnish

Instructions:

1. Sauté tofu in sesame oil until golden.

2. Add snow peas, julienned carrot, and broccoli. Stir-fry until vegetables are tender.

3. Mix in gluten-free soy sauce and rice vinegar.

4. Garnish with sesame seeds before serving.

Preparation Time: 25 minutes

Servings: 2

Nutritional Information:

Calories: 320 | Protein: 18g | Carbohydrates: 25g | Fat: 15g | Fiber: 8g

Vegan Mushroom and Spinach Risotto

Ingredients:

- 1 cup Arborio rice

- 1 cup mushrooms, sliced

- 2 cups fresh spinach

- 1 onion, finely chopped

- 2 cloves garlic, minced

- 1/4 cup nutritional yeast

- 4 cups vegetable broth

Instructions:

1. Sauté chopped onion and minced garlic until translucent.

2. Add sliced mushrooms and cook until tender.

3. Stir in Arborio rice and gradually add vegetable broth, stirring until absorbed.

4. Fold in fresh spinach and nutritional yeast. Continue cooking until rice is creamy.

Preparation Time: 40 minutes

Servings: 4

Nutritional Information:

Calories: 350 | Protein: 8g | Carbohydrates: 70g | Fat: 4g | Fiber: 6g

BBQ Chickpea and Sweet Potato Skewers

Ingredients:

- 1 can (15 oz) chickpeas, drained and rinsed
- 1 large sweet potato, cubed
- 1 red onion, cut into chunks
- 1/2 cup BBQ sauce (gluten-free)
- Wooden skewers, soaked in water

Instructions:

1. Preheat the grill.

2. Thread chickpeas, sweet potato cubes, and red onion chunks onto skewers.

3. Grill until vegetables are tender, brushing with BBQ sauce during cooking.

Preparation Time: 30 minutes

Servings: 2

Nutritional Information:

Calories: 300 | Protein: 10g | Carbohydrates: 55g | Fat: 5g | Fiber: 10g

Quinoa and Broccoli Casserole

Ingredients:

- 1 cup cooked quinoa

- 2 cups broccoli florets

- 1 onion, finely chopped

- 2 cloves garlic, minced

- 1 cup dairy-free shredded cheese

- 1 cup unsweetened almond milk

- 2 tablespoons nutritional yeast

Instructions:

1. Steam broccoli until tender.

2. Sauté chopped onion and minced garlic until softened.

3. In a casserole dish, combine cooked quinoa, steamed broccoli, sautéed onion and garlic, dairy-free shredded cheese, almond milk, and nutritional yeast.

4. Bake at 375°F (190°C) for 20-25 minutes until bubbly and golden.

Preparation Time: 35 minutes

Servings: 4

Nutritional Information:

Calories: 320 | Protein: 15g | Carbohydrates: 40g | Fat: 12g | Fiber: 8g

Thai Red Curry with Tofu and Vegetables

Ingredients:

- 1 block firm tofu, cubed
- 1 cup snap peas
- 1 red bell pepper, sliced
- 1 carrot, thinly sliced
- 2 tablespoons Thai red curry paste
- 1 can (14 oz) coconut milk
- Fresh cilantro for garnish

Instructions:

1. Sauté tofu in a pan until golden.
2. Add snap peas, sliced red bell pepper, and thinly sliced carrot. Cook until vegetables are tender.
3. Stir in Thai red curry paste and pour in coconut milk. Simmer until flavors meld.

4. Garnish with fresh cilantro before serving.

Preparation Time: 30 minutes

Servings: 2

Nutritional Information:

Calories: 380 | Protein: 20g | Carbohydrates: 30g | Fat: 25g | Fiber: 8g

CHAPTER FIVE

GLUTEN, SOY, AND DAIRY-FREE SNACK RECIPES

Carefully Selected Gluten, Soy, and Dairy-Free Snack Recipes

Snacking can be both delicious and nutritious, especially when crafted with a focus on being gluten, soy, and dairy-free. These handpicked recipes ensure a satisfying snack time while accommodating your dietary preferences. Enjoy these flavorful and wholesome snacks guilt-free.

Almond Butter Energy Bites

Ingredients:

- 1 cup gluten-free oats
- 1/2 cup almond butter
- 1/4 cup maple syrup
- 1/4 cup ground flaxseed
- 1 teaspoon vanilla extract
- Pinch of salt

Instructions:

1. In a bowl, mix oats, almond butter, maple syrup, ground flaxseed, vanilla extract, and a pinch of salt.

2. Roll the mixture into bite-sized balls.

3. Refrigerate for 30 minutes before serving.

Preparation Time: 15 minutes

Servings: 12

Nutritional Information:

Calories: 120 | Protein: 4g | Carbohydrates: 15g | Fat: 6g | Fiber: 3g

Roasted Chickpeas

Ingredients:

- 1 can (15 oz) chickpeas, drained and rinsed
- 1 tablespoon olive oil
- 1 teaspoon smoked paprika
- 1/2 teaspoon garlic powder
- Salt and pepper to taste

Instructions:

1. Preheat the oven to 400°F (200°C).

2. Toss chickpeas with olive oil, smoked paprika, garlic powder, salt, and pepper.

3. Spread on a baking sheet and bake for 20-25 minutes until crispy.

Preparation Time: 30 minutes

Servings: 4

Nutritional Information:

Calories: 120 | Protein: 5g | Carbohydrates: 15g | Fat: 4g | Fiber: 4g

Fruit and Nut Trail Mix

Ingredients:

- 1 cup mixed nuts (almonds, walnuts, cashews)

- 1/2 cup dried fruits (cranberries, apricots, raisins)

- 1/4 cup coconut flakes

- 1/4 cup dark chocolate chunks (dairy-free)

Instructions:

1. Mix together mixed nuts, dried fruits, coconut flakes, and dark chocolate chunks.

2. Portion into snack-sized bags for easy grab-and-go.

Preparation Time: 10 minutes

Servings: 6

Nutritional Information:

Calories: 200 | Protein: 5g | Carbohydrates: 15g | Fat: 14g | Fiber: 4g

Guacamole Stuffed Cucumber Bites

Ingredients:

- 2 cucumbers, sliced into rounds

- 2 avocados, mashed

- 1 tomato, diced

- 1/4 cup red onion, finely chopped

- 1 clove garlic, minced

- Lime juice, to taste

- Salt and pepper to taste

Instructions:

1. In a bowl, combine mashed avocados, diced tomato, chopped red onion, minced garlic, lime juice, salt, and pepper.

2. Spoon guacamole onto cucumber rounds.

Preparation Time: 15 minutes

Servings: 4

Nutritional Information:

Calories: 100 | Protein: 2g | Carbohydrates: 8g | Fat: 8g | Fiber: 4g

Rice Cake with Almond Butter and Banana Slices

Ingredients:

- 4 rice cakes (gluten-free)

- 1/2 cup almond butter

- 2 bananas, sliced

- Honey for drizzling (optional)

Instructions:

1. Spread almond butter onto rice cakes.

2. Top with banana slices.

3. Drizzle with honey if desired.

Preparation Time: 10 minutes

Servings: 4

Nutritional Information:

Calories: 180 | Protein: 5g | Carbohydrates: 20g | Fat: 10g | Fiber: 3g

Baked Sweet Potato Chips

Ingredients:

- 2 sweet potatoes, thinly sliced

- 2 tablespoons olive oil

- 1 teaspoon smoked paprika

- 1/2 teaspoon sea salt

Instructions:

1. Preheat the oven to 375°F (190°C).

2. Toss sweet potato slices with olive oil, smoked paprika, and sea salt.

3. Arrange on a baking sheet and bake for 20-25 minutes until crispy.

Preparation Time: 30 minutes

Servings: 4

Nutritional Information:

Calories: 150 | Protein: 2g | Carbohydrates: 20g | Fat: 7g | Fiber: 3g

Hummus and Veggie Snack Plate

Ingredients:

- 1 cup hummus (gluten-free)

- 2 cups mixed veggies (carrots, cucumber, bell peppers)

- Gluten-free crackers

Instructions:

1. Arrange hummus, mixed veggies, and gluten-free crackers on a plate.

2. Dip veggies and crackers into hummus.

Preparation Time: 15 minutes

Servings: 4

Nutritional Information:

Calories: 180 | Protein: 6g | Carbohydrates: 20g | Fat: 10g | Fiber: 6g

Quinoa and Chia Seed Pudding Cups

Ingredients:

- 1 cup cooked quinoa

- 1 cup almond milk (unsweetened)

- 2 tablespoons chia seeds

- 1 tablespoon maple syrup

- Fresh berries for topping

Instructions:

1. In a bowl, mix cooked quinoa, almond milk, chia seeds, and maple syrup.

2. Let it sit in the refrigerator for at least 2 hours or overnight.

3. Spoon into cups and top with fresh berries.

Preparation Time: 10 minutes (plus chilling time)

Servings: 4

Nutritional Information:

Calories: 120 | Protein: 4g | Carbohydrates: 20g | Fat: 4g | Fiber: 5g

Cinnamon Roasted Almonds

Ingredients:

- 2 cups raw almonds
- 1 tablespoon coconut oil, melted
- 1 tablespoon maple syrup
- 1 teaspoon ground cinnamon
- Pinch of sea salt

Instructions:

1. Preheat the oven to 325°F (163°C).

2. In a bowl, coat raw almonds with melted coconut oil, maple syrup, ground cinnamon, and a pinch of sea salt.

3. Spread on a baking sheet and roast for 15-20 minutes, stirring halfway.

Preparation Time: 25 minutes

Servings: 6

Nutritional Information:

Calories: 200 | Protein: 7g | Carbohydrates: 8g | Fat: 16g | Fiber: 4g

Avocado and Salsa Rice Cakes

Ingredients:

- 4 rice cakes (gluten-free)

- 2 avocados, sliced

- 1 cup salsa (dairy-free)

- Fresh cilantro for garnish

Instructions:

1. Place sliced avocado on rice cakes.

2. Spoon salsa over the avocado.

3. Garnish with fresh cilantro.

Preparation Time: 10 minutes

Servings: 4

Nutritional Information:

Calories: 160 | Protein: 2g | Carbohydrates: 20g | Fat: 8g | Fiber: 4g

Pumpkin Spice Energy Balls

Ingredients:

- 1 cup gluten-free rolled oats

- 1/2 cup pumpkin puree

- 1/4 cup almond butter

- 2 tablespoons maple syrup

- 1 teaspoon pumpkin spice

- Shredded coconut for rolling

Instructions:

1. In a bowl, combine rolled oats, pumpkin puree, almond butter, maple syrup, and pumpkin spice.

2. Roll the mixture into bite-sized balls.

3. Roll each ball in shredded coconut.

4. Refrigerate for 30 minutes before serving.

Preparation Time: 20 minutes

Servings: 12

Nutritional Information:

Calories: 110 | Protein: 3g | Carbohydrates: 15g | Fat: 5g | Fiber: 2g

Dairy-Free Spinach Artichoke Dip

Ingredients:

- 1 cup raw cashews, soaked and drained
- 1 cup frozen spinach, thawed and drained
- 1 can (14 oz) artichoke hearts, chopped
- 1/4 cup nutritional yeast
- 2 cloves garlic, minced
- Juice of 1 lemon
- Salt and pepper to taste
- Gluten-free tortilla chips for dipping

Instructions:

1. In a food processor, blend-soaked cashews, thawed spinach, chopped artichoke hearts, nutritional yeast, minced garlic, lemon juice, salt, and pepper until smooth.

2. Serve with gluten-free tortilla chips.

Preparation Time: 15 minutes

Servings: 6

Nutritional Information:

Calories: 160 | Protein: 6g | Carbohydrates: 15g | Fat: 10g | Fiber: 4g

Mango Salsa with Jicama Chips

Ingredients:

- 2 ripe mangos, diced

- 1 red bell pepper, diced

- 1/4 cup red onion, finely chopped

- 1 jalapeño, seeded and minced

- Juice of 2 limes

- 1 jicama, peeled and sliced into chips

Instructions:

1. In a bowl, mix diced mangos, diced red bell pepper, chopped red onion, minced jalapeño, and lime juice.

2. Serve with jicama chips.

Preparation Time: 20 minutes

Servings: 4

Nutritional Information:

Calories: 120 | Protein: 2g | Carbohydrates: 30g | Fat: 1g | Fiber: 8g

Cucumber Roll-Ups with Avocado and Turkey

Ingredients:

- 2 cucumbers, sliced lengthwise

- 1 avocado, mashed

- 8 slices gluten-free turkey

- Fresh dill for garnish

Instructions:

1. Lay cucumber slices flat and spread mashed avocado on each.

2. Place a slice of gluten-free turkey on top.

3. Roll up and secure with a toothpick.

4. Garnish with fresh dill.

Preparation Time: 15 minutes

Servings: 4

Nutritional Information:

Calories: 130 | Protein: 8g | Carbohydrates: 8g | Fat: 8g | Fiber: 4g

Vegan Chocolate Avocado Mousse

Ingredients:

- 2 ripe avocados

- 1/4 cup cocoa powder

- 1/4 cup maple syrup

- 1 teaspoon vanilla extract

- Pinch of sea salt

- Fresh berries for topping

Instructions:

1. In a blender, combine avocados, cocoa powder, maple syrup, vanilla extract, and sea salt until smooth.

2. Spoon into small bowls and top with fresh berries.

Preparation Time: 10 minutes

Servings: 4

Nutritional Information:

Calories: 180 | Protein: 3g | Carbohydrates: 20g | Fat: 12g | Fiber: 6g

Sunflower Seed and Cranberry Bars

Ingredients:

- 1 cup sunflower seed butter

- 1/4 cup honey or agave nectar

- 1 cup gluten-free crispy rice cereal

- 1/2 cup dried cranberries

- 1/4 cup sunflower seeds

Instructions:

1. In a saucepan, melt sunflower seed butter and honey over low heat.

2. Stir in crispy rice cereal, dried cranberries, and sunflower seeds.

3. Press the mixture into a lined baking dish and refrigerate until set.

4. Cut into bars before serving.

Preparation Time: 25 minutes

Servings: 8

Nutritional Information:

Calories: 200 | Protein: 4g | Carbohydrates: 25g | Fat: 10g | Fiber: 3g

Greek Salad Skewers

Ingredients:

- Cherry tomatoes

- Cucumber, cut into chunks

- Kalamata olives

- Dairy-free feta cheese, cubed

- Fresh basil leaves

- Balsamic glaze for drizzling

Instructions:

1. Thread cherry tomatoes, cucumber chunks, Kalamata olives, dairy-free feta cheese cubes, and fresh basil leaves onto skewers.

2. Drizzle with balsamic glaze before serving.

Preparation Time: 15 minutes

Servings: 4

Nutritional Information:

Calories: 120 | Protein: 3g | Carbohydrates: 10g | Fat: 8g | Fiber: 3g

Buffalo Cauliflower Bites

Ingredients:

- 1 small cauliflower, cut into florets
- 1/2 cup gluten-free flour
- 1/2 cup almond milk
- 1 teaspoon garlic powder
- 1 teaspoon onion powder
- 1/2 cup buffalo sauce (gluten-free)
- Dairy-free ranch dressing for dipping

Instructions:

1. Preheat the oven to 450°F (230°C).

2. In a bowl, whisk together gluten-free flour, almond milk, garlic powder, and onion powder.

3. Dip cauliflower florets into the batter, ensuring they are well-coated, and place them on a baking sheet.

4. Bake for 20-25 minutes, then toss with buffalo sauce.

5. Serve with dairy-free ranch dressing.

Preparation Time: 30 minutes

Servings: 4

Nutritional Information:

Calories: 150 | Protein: 4g | Carbohydrates: 20g | Fat: 7g | Fiber: 4g

Apple Nachos

Ingredients:

- 2 apples, thinly sliced
- 1/4 cup almond butter
- 2 tablespoons shredded coconut
- 2 tablespoons chopped nuts (walnuts, almonds)
- 1 tablespoon chia seeds

Instructions:

1. Arrange apple slices on a plate.
2. Drizzle almond butter over the apples.
3. Sprinkle with shredded coconut, chopped nuts, and chia seeds.

Preparation Time: 10 minutes

Servings: 2

Nutritional Information:

Calories: 180 | Protein: 4g | Carbohydrates: 20g | Fat: 10g | Fiber: 6g

Mediterranean Stuffed Mini Peppers

Ingredients:

- Mini sweet peppers, halved and seeded

- Hummus (gluten-free)

- Cherry tomatoes, halved

- Cucumber, diced

- Black olives, sliced

- Fresh parsley for garnish

Instructions:

1. Fill each mini pepper half with a dollop of hummus.

2. Top with cherry tomatoes, diced cucumber, and sliced black olives.

3. Garnish with fresh parsley before serving.

Preparation Time: 20 minutes

Servings: 4

Nutritional Information:

Calories: 100 | Protein: 3g | Carbohydrates: 12g | Fat: 5g | Fiber: 4g

These carefully selected gluten, soy, and dairy-free snack recipes are not only delicious but also cater to your dietary needs. Feel free to indulge in these wholesome treats for a satisfying and guilt-free snacking experience.

CHAPTER SIX

GLUTEN, SOY, AND DAIRY-FREE DESSERT RECIPES

Satisfy your sweet tooth with these carefully chosen dessert recipes, crafted with precision to be both indulgent and compliant with gluten, soy, and dairy-free dietary preferences. Enjoy the delightful flavors without compromising your health-conscious choices.

Flourless Chocolate Avocado Brownies

Ingredients:

- 2 ripe avocados, mashed

- 1/2 cup maple syrup

- 1 teaspoon vanilla extract

- 3/4 cup cocoa powder

- 1/2 cup almond flour

- 1/2 teaspoon baking powder

- Pinch of salt

- Dairy-free chocolate chips for topping

Instructions:

1. Preheat the oven to 350°F (175°C) and grease a baking pan.

2. In a bowl, combine mashed avocados, maple syrup, and vanilla extract.

3. Add cocoa powder, almond flour, baking powder, and a pinch of salt. Mix until smooth.

4. Pour the batter into the prepared pan, sprinkle with dairy-free chocolate chips, and bake for 25-30 minutes.

5. Allow to cool before cutting into squares.

Preparation Time: 35 minutes

Servings: 12

Nutritional Information:

Calories: 150 | Protein: 3g | Carbohydrates: 20g | Fat: 8g | Fiber: 5g

Vegan Raspberry Almond Tart

Ingredients:

- 1 cup almond flour

- 1/4 cup coconut oil, melted

- 2 tablespoons maple syrup

- 1 cup fresh raspberries

- 1/2 cup almond butter

- 2 tablespoons coconut milk

- 1 tablespoon maple syrup (for the filling)

Instructions:

1. In a bowl, combine almond flour, melted coconut oil, and maple syrup to create the crust.

2. Press the mixture into a tart pan and refrigerate for 30 minutes.

3. In a separate bowl, mix almond butter, coconut milk, and maple syrup for the filling.

4. Spread the filling over the crust and top with fresh raspberries.

5. Chill for an additional 1-2 hours before serving.

Preparation Time: 45 minutes

Servings: 8

Nutritional Information:

Calories: 180 | Protein: 5g | Carbohydrates: 12g | Fat: 14g | Fiber: 4g

Coconut Mango Chia Pudding

Ingredients:

- 1/4 cup chia seeds
- 1 cup coconut milk (unsweetened)
- 1 tablespoon maple syrup
- 1/2 teaspoon vanilla extract
- 1 ripe mango, diced

Instructions:

1. In a bowl, mix chia seeds, coconut milk, maple syrup, and vanilla extract.

2. Refrigerate for at least 4 hours or overnight.

3. Layer the chia pudding with diced mango in serving glasses.

4. Garnish with additional mango before serving.

Preparation Time: 5 minutes (plus chilling time)

Servings: 2

Nutritional Information:

Calories: 180 | Protein: 4g | Carbohydrates: 25g | Fat: 8g | Fiber: 8g

No-Bake Almond Joy Energy Bites

Ingredients:

- 1 cup gluten-free rolled oats

- 1/2 cup almond butter

- 1/4 cup maple syrup

- 1/4 cup shredded coconut (unsweetened)

- 1/4 cup dairy-free chocolate chips

- 1/4 cup chopped almonds

Instructions:

1. In a food processor, blend rolled oats, almond butter, maple syrup, shredded coconut, dairy-free chocolate chips, and chopped almonds.

2. Roll the mixture into bite-sized balls and refrigerate for 30 minutes before serving.

Preparation Time: 15 minutes

Servings: 12

Nutritional Information:

Calories: 120 | Protein: 3g | Carbohydrates: 15g | Fat: 6g | Fiber: 3g

Paleo Lemon Blueberry Bars

Ingredients:

- 2 cups almond flour
- 1/4 cup coconut flour
- 1/2 cup coconut oil, melted
- 1/3 cup maple syrup
- 1 teaspoon vanilla extract
- Zest and juice of 2 lemons
- 1 cup fresh blueberries

Instructions:

1. Preheat the oven to 350°F (175°C) and line a baking dish with parchment paper.

2. In a bowl, combine almond flour, coconut flour, melted coconut oil, maple syrup, vanilla extract, lemon zest, and lemon juice.

3. Press the mixture into the prepared dish, then evenly distribute fresh blueberries on top.

4. Bake for 25-30 minutes until the edges are golden brown.

5. Allow to cool before cutting into bars.

Preparation Time: 40 minutes

Servings: 9

Nutritional Information:

Calories: 220 | Protein: 5g | Carbohydrates: 20g | Fat: 15g | Fiber: 4g

Chocolate Banana Ice Cream

Ingredients:

- 4 ripe bananas, sliced and frozen

- 2 tablespoons cocoa powder

- 1/4 cup almond milk (unsweetened)

- 1 teaspoon vanilla extract

- Dairy-free chocolate chips for topping

Instructions:

1. In a blender, combine frozen banana slices, cocoa powder, almond milk, and vanilla extract.

2. Blend until smooth, scraping down the sides as needed.

3. Transfer to a bowl, top with dairy-free chocolate chips, and enjoy immediately.

Preparation Time: 10 minutes

Servings: 4

Calories: 120 | Protein: 2g | Carbohydrates: 30g | Fat: 1g | Fiber: 4g

Vegan Pumpkin Pie Pudding

Ingredients:

- 1 can (15 oz) pumpkin puree
- 1/2 cup coconut milk (full-fat)
- 1/4 cup maple syrup
- 1 teaspoon pumpkin pie spice
- 1 teaspoon vanilla extract
- 1/4 cup chopped pecans for topping

Instructions:

1. In a bowl, whisk together pumpkin puree, coconut milk, maple syrup, pumpkin pie spice, and vanilla extract.

2. Refrigerate for at least 2 hours.

3. Spoon into serving bowls, top with chopped pecans, and serve.

Preparation Time: 10 minutes (plus chilling time)

Servings: 4

Nutritional Information:

Calories: 150 | Protein: 2g | Carbohydrates: 20g | Fat: 8g | Fiber: 5g

Coconut Flour Chocolate Chip Cookies

Ingredients:

- 1/2 cup coconut flour
- 1/4 cup coconut oil, melted
- 1/4 cup maple syrup
- 2 flax eggs (2 tablespoons flaxseed meal + 5 tablespoons water)
- 1 teaspoon vanilla extract
- 1/2 cup dairy-free chocolate chips

Instructions:

1. Preheat the oven to 350°F (175°C) and line a baking sheet with parchment paper.
2. In a bowl, mix coconut flour, melted coconut oil, maple syrup, flax eggs, and vanilla extract.
3. Fold in dairy-free chocolate chips.
4. Form into cookies and place on the prepared baking sheet.
5. Bake for 12-15 minutes until the edges are golden brown.

Preparation Time: 20 minutes

Servings: 12

Nutritional Information:

Calories: 120 | Protein: 2g | Carbohydrates: 15g | Fat: 7g | Fiber: 3g

Dairy-Free Matcha Chia Seed Pudding

Ingredients:

- 1/4 cup chia seeds
- 1 cup coconut milk (unsweetened)
- 1 tablespoon maple syrup
- 1 teaspoon matcha powder
- Fresh berries for topping

Instructions:

1. In a bowl, combine chia seeds, coconut milk, maple syrup, and matcha powder.
2. Refrigerate for at least 4 hours or overnight.
3. Spoon into serving glasses and top with fresh berries.

Preparation Time: 5 minutes (plus chilling time)

Servings: 2

Nutritional Information:

Calories: 160 | Protein: 4g | Carbohydrates: 20g | Fat: 8g | Fiber: 8g

Gluten-Free Vegan Apple Crisp

Ingredients:

- 4 cups apples, peeled and sliced
- 1 tablespoon lemon juice
- 1/4 cup maple syrup

- 1 teaspoon ground cinnamon

- 1/2 cup gluten-free rolled oats

- 1/4 cup almond flour

- 2 tablespoons coconut oil, melted

- 2 tablespoons chopped pecans

Instructions:

1. Preheat the oven to 350°F (175°C) and grease a baking dish.

2. In a bowl, toss sliced apples with lemon juice, maple syrup, and ground cinnamon. Transfer to the prepared baking dish.

3. In a separate bowl, combine rolled oats, almond flour, melted coconut oil, and chopped pecans.

4. Sprinkle the oat mixture over the apples.

5. Bake for 30-35 minutes until the top is golden brown.

6. Allow to cool slightly before serving.

Preparation Time: 45 minutes

Servings: 6

Nutritional Information:

Calories: 180 | Protein: 3g | Carbohydrates: 30g | Fat: 7g | Fiber: 5g

Quinoa Chocolate Pudding Parfait

Ingredients:

- 1 cup cooked quinoa

- 1/4 cup cocoa powder

- 1/4 cup maple syrup

- 1 teaspoon vanilla extract

- 1 cup coconut yogurt (dairy-free)

- Fresh berries for layering

Instructions:

1. In a bowl, mix cooked quinoa, cocoa powder, maple syrup, and vanilla extract.

2. In serving glasses, layer quinoa mixture with coconut yogurt and fresh berries.

3. Repeat the layers and refrigerate for at least 2 hours before serving.

Preparation Time: 15 minutes (plus chilling time)

Servings: 4

Nutritional Information:

Calories: 200 | Protein: 5g | Carbohydrates: 30g | Fat: 8g | Fiber: 5g

Dairy-Free Chocolate Mousse

Ingredients:

- 2 ripe avocados

- 1/4 cup cocoa powder

- 1/4 cup maple syrup

- 1 teaspoon vanilla extract

- Pinch of sea salt

- Dairy-free whipped cream for topping

Instructions:

1. In a blender, combine avocados, cocoa powder, maple syrup, vanilla extract, and a pinch of sea salt.

2. Blend until smooth and creamy.

3. Spoon into serving cups and refrigerate for 1-2 hours.

4. Top with dairy-free whipped cream before serving.

Preparation Time: 10 minutes (plus chilling time)

Servings: 4

Nutritional Information:

Calories: 180 | Protein: 3g | Carbohydrates: 25g | Fat: 10g | Fiber: 6g

Gluten-Free Vegan Banana Bread

Ingredients:

- 3 ripe bananas, mashed

- 1/4 cup coconut oil, melted

- 1/4 cup maple syrup

- 1 teaspoon vanilla extract

- 2 cups gluten-free flour

- 1 teaspoon baking soda

- 1/2 teaspoon cinnamon

- 1/4 cup chopped walnuts

Instructions:

1. Preheat the oven to 350°F (175°C) and grease a loaf pan.

2. In a bowl, mix mashed bananas, melted coconut oil, maple syrup, and vanilla extract.

3. Add gluten-free flour, baking soda, cinnamon, and chopped walnuts. Stir until combined.

4. Pour the batter into the prepared pan and bake for 50-60 minutes.

5. Allow to cool before slicing.

Preparation Time: 70 minutes

Servings: 10

Nutritional Information:

Calories: 220 | Protein: 3g | Carbohydrates: 35g | Fat: 8g | Fiber: 4g

Raspberry Coconut Chia Seed Popsicles

Ingredients:

- 1 cup coconut milk (unsweetened)

- 1 cup fresh raspberries

- 2 tablespoons maple syrup

- 2 tablespoons chia seeds

Instructions:

1. In a blender, combine coconut milk, fresh raspberries, maple syrup, and chia seeds.

2. Blend until smooth.

3. Pour the mixture into popsicle molds and freeze for at least 4 hours.

Preparation Time: 10 minutes (plus freezing time)

Servings: 6

Nutritional Information:

Calories: 90 | Protein: 2g | Carbohydrates: 10g | Fat: 5g | Fiber: 4g

Chocolate Covered Strawberry Bliss Balls

Ingredients:

- 1 cup gluten-free rolled oats
- 1/2 cup dried strawberries
- 1/4 cup almond butter
- 2 tablespoons cocoa powder
- 2 tablespoons maple syrup
- Dairy-free chocolate for coating

Instructions:

1. In a food processor, blend rolled oats, dried strawberries, almond butter, cocoa powder, and maple syrup until a dough forms.

2. Roll the mixture into bite-sized balls.

3. Melt dairy-free chocolate and dip each ball to coat.

4. Place on parchment paper and refrigerate until the chocolate sets.

Preparation Time: 20 minutes

Servings: 12

Nutritional Information:

Calories: 130 | Protein: 3g | Carbohydrates: 18g | Fat: 6g | Fiber: 3g

Almond Flour Lemon Poppy Seed Cookies

Ingredients:

- 2 cups almond flour

- 1/4 cup coconut oil, melted

- 1/4 cup maple syrup

- Zest and juice of 2 lemons

- 1 teaspoon vanilla extract

- 1 tablespoon poppy seeds

Instructions:

1. Preheat the oven to 350°F (175°C) and line a baking sheet with parchment paper.

2. In a bowl, mix almond flour, melted coconut oil, maple syrup, lemon zest, lemon juice, vanilla extract, and poppy seeds.

3. Scoop tablespoon-sized portions onto the prepared baking sheet.

4. Bake for 12-15 minutes until the edges are golden brown.

Preparation Time: 25 minutes

Servings: 12

Nutritional Information:

Calories: 150 | Protein: 4g | Carbohydrates: 10g | Fat: 12g | Fiber: 3g

Dairy-Free Mango Sorbet

Ingredients:

- 3 cups frozen mango chunks

- 1/4 cup coconut milk (unsweetened)

- 2 tablespoons maple syrup

- 1 tablespoon lime juice

Instructions:

1. In a blender, combine frozen mango chunks, coconut milk, maple syrup, and lime juice.

2. Blend until smooth, scraping down the sides as needed.

3. Transfer to a container and freeze for at least 2 hours.

4. Scoop and enjoy!

Preparation Time: 10 minutes (plus freezing time)

Servings: 4

Nutritional Information:

Calories: 120 | Protein: 2g | Carbohydrates: 30g | Fat: 1g | Fiber: 3g

Hazelnut Chocolate Banana Bites

Ingredients:

- 2 ripe bananas, sliced

- 2 tablespoons hazelnut butter

- Dairy-free chocolate for drizzling

- Chopped hazelnuts for topping

Instructions:

1. Spread hazelnut butter on banana slices.

2. Sandwich two slices together and place on a parchment-lined tray.

3. Drizzle with melted dairy-free chocolate and sprinkle chopped hazelnuts.

4. Freeze for 1-2 hours before serving.

Preparation Time: 15 minutes (plus freezing time)

Servings: 4

Nutritional Information:

Calories: 160 | Protein: 2g | Carbohydrates: 25g | Fat: 8g | Fiber: 3g

Blueberry Coconut Rice Pudding

Ingredients:

- 1 cup cooked brown rice
- 1 cup coconut milk (unsweetened)
- 1/4 cup maple syrup
- 1/2 cup fresh blueberries
- 1/4 cup shredded coconut (unsweetened)

Instructions:

1. In a saucepan, combine cooked brown rice, coconut milk, and maple syrup.
2. Simmer over low heat until the mixture thickens.
3. Stir in fresh blueberries and shredded coconut.
4. Serve warm or chilled.

Preparation Time: 20 minutes

Servings: 4

Nutritional Information:

Calories: 180 | Protein: 3g | Carbohydrates: 30g | Fat: 7g | Fiber: 4g

Vegan Chocolate Pomegranate Cups

Ingredients:

- 1 cup dairy-free chocolate chips

- 1/2 cup pomegranate arils

Instructions:

1. Melt dairy-free chocolate chips in a microwave-safe bowl.

2. Line a mini muffin tin with paper liners.

3. Spoon a small amount of melted chocolate into each cup, covering the bottom.

4. Drop a few pomegranate arils into each cup.

5. Cover with more melted chocolate.

6. Refrigerate until set.

Preparation Time: 15 minutes (plus chilling time)

Servings: 8

Nutritional Information:

Calories: 130 | Protein: 1g | Carbohydrates: 15g | Fat: 8g | Fiber: 2g

These thoughtfully selected gluten, soy, and dairy-free dessert recipes ensure that you can enjoy the sweetness of life while adhering to your dietary preferences. Delight in these treats, knowing they are crafted with care for both your taste buds and your well-being.

CHAPTER SEVEN

GLUTEN, SOY, AND DAIRY-FREE BEVERAGE RECIPES

Quench your thirst with these carefully curated beverage recipes, designed to cater to gluten, soy, and dairy-free dietary preferences. Each sip is a symphony of flavors, ensuring a delightful and refreshing experience without compromising your health-conscious choices.

Tropical Green Smoothie

Ingredients:

- 1 cup kale, stems removed
- 1/2 cup pineapple chunks
- 1/2 banana
- 1/2 cup coconut water
- 1 tablespoon chia seeds
- Ice cubes

Instructions:

1. In a blender, combine kale, pineapple chunks, banana, coconut water, and chia seeds.
2. Blend until smooth.
3. Add ice cubes and blend again until desired consistency.
4. Pour into a glass and enjoy!

Preparation Time: 7 minutes

Servings: 1

Nutritional Information:

Calories: 150 | Protein: 4g | Carbohydrates: 30g | Fat: 5g | Fiber: 8g

Golden Turmeric Latte

Ingredients:

- 1 cup almond milk (unsweetened)

- 1 teaspoon turmeric powder

- 1/2 teaspoon cinnamon

- 1/4 teaspoon ginger powder

- 1 tablespoon maple syrup

- Pinch of black pepper

Instructions:

1. In a saucepan, heat almond milk over medium heat.

2. Whisk in turmeric powder, cinnamon, ginger powder, maple syrup, and a pinch of black pepper.

3. Continue to whisk until heated through but not boiling.

4. Pour into a mug and savor the warmth.

Preparation Time: 5 minutes

Servings: 1

Nutritional Information:

Calories: 80 | Protein: 2g | Carbohydrates: 15g | Fat: 3g | Fiber: 2g

Berry Beet Detox Juice

Ingredients:

- 1 cup mixed berries (strawberries, blueberries, raspberries)
- 1 small beet, peeled and chopped
- 1/2 cucumber, sliced
- 1 tablespoon fresh lemon juice
- 1 cup coconut water

Instructions:

1. In a juicer, process mixed berries, beet, cucumber, and fresh lemon juice.
2. Pour the juice into a glass and top with coconut water.
3. Stir well and enjoy the vibrant detoxification.

Preparation Time: 10 minutes

Servings: 1

Nutritional Information:

Calories: 120 | Protein: 3g | Carbohydrates: 25g | Fat: 1g | Fiber: 8g

Iced Vanilla Almond Chai Latte

Ingredients:

- 1 cup brewed chai tea, chilled

- 1/2 cup almond milk (unsweetened)

- 1 teaspoon vanilla extract

- Ice cubes

- Optional: sweeten with maple syrup

Instructions:

1. In a glass, combine chilled brewed chai tea, almond milk, vanilla extract, and ice cubes.

2. Stir well.

3. Sweeten with maple syrup if desired.

4. Sip and revel in the soothing flavors.

Preparation Time: 5 minutes

Servings: 1

Nutritional Information:

Calories: 30 | Protein: 1g | Carbohydrates: 5g | Fat: 1g | Fiber: 1g

Cucumber Mint Cooler

Ingredients:

- 1 cucumber, sliced

- Handful of fresh mint leaves

- 1 tablespoon fresh lime juice

- 2 cups sparkling water

- Ice cubes

Instructions:

1. In a pitcher, combine cucumber slices, fresh mint leaves, and lime juice.

2. Muddle the ingredients to release flavors.

3. Add sparkling water and stir gently.

4. Pour over ice and relish the crispness.

Preparation Time: 8 minutes

Servings: 2

Nutritional Information:

Calories: 10 | Protein: 0g | Carbohydrates: 2g | Fat: 0g | Fiber: 1g

Pineapple Ginger Elixir

Ingredients:

- 1 cup fresh pineapple chunks

- 1-inch piece of ginger, peeled and sliced

- 1 tablespoon fresh lemon juice

- 2 cups coconut water

- Ice cubes

Instructions:

1. In a blender, blend fresh pineapple chunks, sliced ginger, fresh lemon juice, and coconut water.

2. Strain the mixture into a glass.

3. Serve over ice for a revitalizing tropical treat.

Preparation Time: 6 minutes

Servings: 1

Nutritional Information:

Calories: 80 | Protein: 1g | Carbohydrates: 20g | Fat: 0g | Fiber: 2g

Matcha Coconut Frappe

Ingredients:

- 1 teaspoon matcha powder

- 1 cup coconut milk (unsweetened)

- 1 tablespoon maple syrup

- 1/2 teaspoon vanilla extract

- Ice cubes

Instructions:

1. In a blender, combine matcha powder, coconut milk, maple syrup, and vanilla extract.

2. Add ice cubes and blend until smooth.

3. Pour into a glass and savor the energizing matcha goodness.

Preparation Time: 5 minutes

Servings: 1

Nutritional Information:

Calories: 90 | Protein: 2g | Carbohydrates: 15g | Fat: 4g | Fiber: 1g

Watermelon Mint Refresher

Ingredients:

- 2 cups fresh watermelon, cubed

- Handful of fresh mint leaves

- 1 tablespoon fresh lime juice

- 1 cup coconut water

- Ice cubes

Instructions:

1. In a blender, blend fresh watermelon cubes, mint leaves, lime juice, and coconut water.

2. Strain the mixture into a pitcher.

3. Serve over ice for a hydrating and cooling sensation.

Preparation Time: 7 minutes

Servings: 2

Nutritional Information:

Calories: 60 | Protein: 1g | Carbohydrates: 15g | Fat: 0g | Fiber: 1g

Blueberry Basil Lemonade

Ingredients:

- 1 cup fresh blueberries

- Handful of fresh basil leaves

- 1 tablespoon fresh lemon juice

- 2 cups still or sparkling water

- Ice cubes

Instructions:

1. In a blender, blend fresh blueberries, basil leaves, and fresh lemon juice.

2. Strain the mixture into a pitcher.

3. Add still or sparkling water and stir.

4. Pour over ice and relish the berry-infused lemonade.

Preparation Time: 8 minutes

Servings: 2

Nutritional Information:

Calories: 30 | Protein: 1g | Carbohydrates: 7g | Fat: 0g | Fiber: 2g

Apple Cinnamon Spice Tea

Ingredients:

- 1 apple, sliced

- 2 cinnamon sticks

- 1 tablespoon loose leaf black tea or 2 tea bags

- 2 cups hot water

- Optional: sweeten with maple syrup

Instructions:

1. In a teapot, combine apple slices, cinnamon sticks, and black tea.

2. Pour hot water over the ingredients and steep for 5-7 minutes.

3. Strain into cups and sweeten with maple syrup if desired.

4. Embrace the comforting warmth of apple and cinnamon.

Preparation Time: 10 minutes

Servings: 2

Nutritional Information:

Calories: 15 | Protein: 0g | Carbohydrates: 4g | Fat: 0g | Fiber: 1g

Chilled Lavender Lemonade

Ingredients:

- 2 tablespoons dried lavender buds

- 1 cup hot water

- 1/4 cup fresh lemon juice

- 2 tablespoons agave nectar

- 2 cups cold water

- Ice cubes

Instructions:

1. Steep dried lavender buds in hot water for 10 minutes to make lavender tea.

2. Strain the tea into a pitcher and add fresh lemon juice, agave nectar, and cold water.

3. Stir well and refrigerate until chilled.

4. Serve over ice for a calming and refreshing lavender lemonade.

Preparation Time: 15 minutes (plus chilling time)

Servings: 2

Nutritional Information:

Calories: 40 | Protein: 0g | Carbohydrates: 10g | Fat: 0g | Fiber: 0g

Minty Watermelon Lime Splash

Ingredients:

- 2 cups fresh watermelon, cubed

- Handful of fresh mint leaves

- 1 tablespoon fresh lime juice

- 1 cup coconut water

- Sparkling water (optional)

- Ice cubes

Instructions:

1. In a blender, blend fresh watermelon cubes, mint leaves, lime juice, and coconut water.

2. Strain the mixture into a pitcher.

3. Add sparkling water if desired and stir gently.

4. Pour over ice and revel in the minty watermelon bliss.

Preparation Time: 8 minutes

Servings: 2

Nutritional Information:

Calories: 50 | Protein: 1g | Carbohydrates: 12g | Fat: 0g | Fiber: 1g

Raspberry Hibiscus Iced Tea

Ingredients:

- 2 hibiscus tea bags

- 1 cup hot water

- 1/2 cup fresh raspberries

- 1 tablespoon agave nectar

- Ice cubes

Instructions:

1. Steep hibiscus tea bags in hot water for 5-7 minutes.

2. In a blender, blend fresh raspberries and agave nectar.

3. Strain the hibiscus tea into a pitcher and add the raspberry mixture.

4. Stir well and refrigerate until chilled.

5. Serve over ice for a vibrant and fruity iced tea.

Preparation Time: 12 minutes (plus chilling time)

Servings: 2

Nutritional Information:

Calories: 30 | Protein: 1g | Carbohydrates: 7g | Fat: 0g | Fiber: 4g

Energizing Green Tea Smoothie

Ingredients:

- 1 green tea bag

- 1 cup hot water

- 1/2 cup pineapple chunks

- 1/2 banana

- 1/2 cup almond milk (unsweetened)

- 1 tablespoon chia seeds

- Ice cubes

Instructions:

1. Steep the green tea bag in hot water for 3-5 minutes.

2. Remove the tea bag and let the tea cool.

3. In a blender, combine green tea, pineapple chunks, banana, almond milk, and chia seeds.

4. Blend until smooth.

5. Add ice cubes and blend again until desired consistency.

6. Pour into a glass and enjoy the green tea boost.

Preparation Time: 10 minutes (plus cooling time)

Servings: 1

Nutritional Information:

Calories: 120 | Protein: 3g | Carbohydrates: 25g | Fat: 2g | Fiber: 8g

Pineapple Basil Sparkler

Ingredients:

- 1 cup fresh pineapple juice

- Handful of fresh basil leaves

- 1 tablespoon fresh lime juice

- 2 cups sparkling water

- Ice cubes

Instructions:

1. In a pitcher, combine fresh pineapple juice, basil leaves, and fresh lime juice.

2. Muddle the basil leaves to release flavors.

3. Add sparkling water and stir gently.

4. Pour over ice and relish the tropical basil infusion.

Preparation Time: 7 minutes

Servings: 2

Nutritional Information:

Calories: 50 | Protein: 1g | Carbohydrates: 12g | Fat: 0g | Fiber: 1g

Detoxifying Ginger Lemon Elixir

Ingredients:

- 1 tablespoon fresh ginger, grated

- 1 tablespoon fresh lemon juice

- 1 tablespoon agave nectar

- 2 cups hot water

- Optional: a pinch of cayenne pepper

- Ice cubes

Instructions:

1. In a mug, combine grated fresh ginger, fresh lemon juice, and agave nectar.

2. Pour hot water over the ingredients and let it steep for 5 minutes.

3. Optionally, add a pinch of cayenne pepper for an extra kick.

4. Strain into a glass over ice and enjoy the detoxifying elixir.

Preparation Time: 8 minutes

Servings: 1

Nutritional Information:

Calories: 20 | Protein: 0g | Carbohydrates: 5g | Fat: 0g | Fiber: 0g

Peach Basil Iced Tea

Ingredients:

- 2 peach tea bags
- 1 cup hot water
- Handful of fresh basil leaves
- 1 tablespoon agave nectar
- Ice cubes

Instructions:

1. Steep peach tea bags in hot water for 5-7 minutes.

2. In a pitcher, combine hot peach tea, fresh basil leaves, and agave nectar.

3. Stir well and let it cool in the refrigerator.

4. Serve over ice for a delightful peach and basil iced tea.

Preparation Time: 12 minutes (plus chilling time)

Servings: 2

Nutritional Information:

Calories: 30 | Protein: 0g | Carbohydrates: 8g | Fat: 0g | Fiber: 1g

Citrusy Mango Tango Smoothie

Ingredients:

- 1/2 cup mango chunks

- 1/2 orange, peeled

- 1/2 banana

- 1/2 cup coconut milk (unsweetened)

- 1 tablespoon flaxseeds

- Ice cubes

Instructions:

1. In a blender, combine mango chunks, peeled orange, banana, coconut milk, and flaxseeds.

2. Blend until smooth.

3. Add ice cubes and blend again until desired consistency.

4. Pour into a glass and enjoy the citrusy mango tango.

Preparation Time: 7 minutes

Servings: 1

Nutritional Information:

Calories: 150 | Protein: 3g | Carbohydrates: 30g | Fat: 5g | Fiber: 5g

Blueberry Lavender Lemon Sparkle

Ingredients:

- 1 cup blueberries

- 1 tablespoon dried lavender buds

- 1 tablespoon fresh lemon juice

- 2 cups sparkling water

- Ice cubes

Instructions:

1. In a blender, blend blueberries, dried lavender buds, and fresh lemon juice.

2. Strain the mixture into a pitcher.

3. Add sparkling water and stir gently.

4. Pour over ice and enjoy the blueberry lavender sparkle.

Preparation Time: 10 minutes

Servings: 2

Nutritional Information:

Calories: 40 | Protein: 1g | Carbohydrates: 10g | Fat: 0g | Fiber: 2g

Hibiscus Mint Cooler

Ingredients:

- 2 hibiscus tea bags

- 1 cup hot water

- Handful of fresh mint leaves

- 1 tablespoon agave nectar

- 2 cups cold water

- Ice cubes

Instructions:

1. Steep hibiscus tea bags in hot water for 5-7 minutes.

2. In a pitcher, combine hot hibiscus tea, fresh mint leaves, and agave nectar.

3. Stir well and let it cool in the refrigerator.

4. Serve over ice for a revitalizing hibiscus mint cooler.

Preparation Time: 12 minutes (plus chilling time)

Servings: 2

Nutritional Information:

Calories: 30 | Protein: 0g | Carbohydrates: 8g | Fat: 0g | Fiber: 1g

These thoughtfully crafted gluten, soy, and dairy-free beverage recipes are not only refreshing but also align with your commitment to a health-conscious lifestyle. Enjoy the diverse flavors, from tropical greens to comforting spices, as you elevate your beverage experience. Cheers to both taste and well-being!

CONCLUSION

Embarking on a journey toward a gluten, soy, and dairy-free lifestyle is not merely a dietary shift but a holistic commitment to well-being. Throughout our exploration, we have delved into the intricacies of gluten, soy, and dairy, understanding their potential impact on those with allergies or sensitivities. The need for conscientious food choices has led us to the creation of a comprehensive cookbook, brimming with meticulously selected recipes to cater to these dietary preferences.

Our cookbook not only addresses health concerns but also celebrates the richness of a varied and flavorful diet. From breakfast to dinner, snacks to desserts, and beverages to elixirs, each recipe is a testament to the diverse and delicious possibilities available within the realm of gluten, soy, and dairy-free cuisine. Carefully curated, these recipes ensure that individuals can savor meals without compromising taste or nutritional value.

Navigating the aisles with a gluten, soy, and dairy-free shopping list becomes an empowering experience, armed with the knowledge of alternative ingredients that foster a thriving and nourishing lifestyle. The inclusion of wholesome options such as fruits, vegetables, lean proteins, and gluten-free grains not only caters to dietary restrictions but also promotes overall health and vitality.

The journey doesn't end at the supermarket; it extends to the kitchen, where smart cooking tips facilitate the creation of delectable dishes.

These tips, ranging from ingredient substitutions to mindful preparation techniques, empower individuals to embrace the culinary arts with confidence and creativity. Cooking becomes an enjoyable endeavor, marked by the joy of crafting meals that align with personal health goals.

Our culinary exploration further extends into the realm of meal planning, with carefully designed recipes for breakfast, lunch, dinner, snacks, and desserts. Each dish, infused with a thoughtful selection of ingredients, not only caters to dietary needs but also boasts a nutritional profile that promotes overall wellness. From the vibrant colors of fresh vegetables to the rich flavors of alternative flours, our recipes inspire a newfound appreciation for the diversity of gluten, soy, and dairy-free ingredients.

As we savor the culinary delights crafted from these recipes, we recognize that embracing a gluten, soy, and dairy-free lifestyle goes beyond a dietary adjustment. It becomes a celebration of nourishing the body, indulging the taste buds, and fostering a sense of well-being. The journey is not restrictive; it is an invitation to explore, experiment, and relish the abundance of flavors that nature provides.

In the realm of gluten, soy, and dairy-free living, our cookbook serves as a guiding light, offering a roadmap for individuals seeking flavorful alternatives. It champions the idea that dietary restrictions need not hinder the enjoyment of food but rather open doors to a world of culinary possibilities. With each carefully crafted recipe, we encourage a mindset shift—from viewing dietary restrictions as limitations to embracing them as an opportunity for culinary innovation and creativity.

In the words of the renowned chef and author, Julia Child, "The only time to eat diet food is while you're waiting for the steak to cook." This quote encapsulates the essence of our culinary journey—a reminder that while dietary choices are significant, they should never detract from the sheer joy and pleasure that food brings to our lives. Our cookbook, filled with gluten, soy, and dairy-free recipes, invites you to savor every moment in the kitchen, appreciating not only the nutritional value of the ingredients but also the artistry of creating meals that nourish the body and delight the senses.

As we close the chapter on our discussion, let these recipes be a source of inspiration, empowerment, and culinary adventure. May each dish you create be a testament to the joy of conscious living and the celebration of a vibrant, gluten, soy, and dairy-free lifestyle.

Made in the USA
Monee, IL
21 December 2024

74973838R00085